Student Problem Manual

for use with

Investments

Eighth Edition

Zvi Bodie
Boston University

Alex Kane
University of California – San Diego

Alan J. Marcus
Boston College

Prepared by
Larry Prather
Southeastern Oklahoma State University

McGraw-Hill
Irwin

Boston   Burr Ridge, IL   Dubuque, IA   New York   San Francisco   St. Louis
Bangkok   Bogotá   Caracas   Kuala Lumpur   Lisbon   London   Madrid   Mexico City
Milan   Montreal   New Delhi   Santiago   Seoul   Singapore   Sydney   Taipei   Toronto

Student Problem Manual for use with
INVESTMENTS
Zvi Bodie, Alex Kane, and Alan J. Marcus

Published by McGraw-Hill/Irwin, an imprint of The McGraw-Hill Companies, Inc., 1221 Avenue of the Americas, New York, NY 10020. Copyright © 2009, 2008, 2005 by The McGraw-Hill Companies, Inc. All rights reserved.

1 2 3 4 5 6 7 8 9 0 BKM/BKM 0 9 8

ISBN: 978-0-07-336356-1
MHID: 0-07-336356-1

www.mhhe.com

TABLE OF CONTENTS

Answers

VI.   Options, Futures, and Other Derivatives

VII.   Applied Portfolio Management

Chapter 1
The Investment Environment

1. What is a real asset?

2. What is a financial asset?

3. Classify the following examples of investments as fixed-income, equity, or derivative.
   a. a share of Google common stock
   b. a Treasury bond
   c. a call option on Texas Instruments stock
   d. an IBM bond
   e. a gold futures contract
   f. a share of stock in a closely held corporation

4. Complete the following items as they relate to the aggregate Balance Sheet of U.S. Households.
   a. Real assets make up _____% of total assets.
   b. Financial assets make up _____% of total assets.
   c. The largest component of real assets is _____.
   d. The four largest components of financial assets are _____, _____, _____, and _____.
   e. The largest component of liabilities is _____.
   f. The net worth percentage is _____.

5. What is consumption timing and why is it important?

6. What is allocation of risk and why is it important?

7. What is separation of ownership and management and why is it important?

8. What is the "agency problem"? What are some possible solutions to the problem?

9. What are the three sectors of the economy and what are their primary needs?

10. Give three examples of specific types of financial intermediaries. List and explain four important functions that financial intermediaries perform.

11. Complete the following items as they relate to the aggregate Balance Sheet of U.S. Commercial Banks.
    a. Real (tangible) assets make up _____% of total assets.
    b. Financial assets make up _____% of total assets.
    c. The largest component of real assets is _____.
    d. The two largest components of financial assets are _____ and _____.
    e. The two largest components of liabilities are ____ and _____.
    f. The net worth percentage is _____.

12. Complete the following items as they relate to the aggregate Balance Sheet of Nonfinancial U.S. Businesses.
    a. Real assets make up _____% of total assets.
    b. Financial assets make up _____% of total assets.
    c. The two largest components of real assets are _____ and _____.
    d. The two largest components of financial assets are _____ and _____.
    e. The two largest components of liabilities are ____ and _____.
    f. The net worth percentage is _____.

13. Define the term "securitization". Give two examples of investments that have been securitized.

14. What is the difference between a primary market transaction and a secondary market transaction?

15. List and briefly explain five ways an investor can diversify globally.

16. What is the difference between asset allocation and security selection?

17. What are the two portfolio construction methods and how do they differ?

Chapter 2
Asset Classes and Financial Instruments

1. Match the following investments with their definitions.
    T-bill
    Eurodollar
    Repurchase Agreement
    Commercial Paper
    Bankers' Acceptance
    Federal Funds

    a. short-term sale of government securities with an agreement to repurchase them at a higher price
    b. funds in the accounts of commercial banks at the Federal Reserve Bank
    c. short-term unsecured debt issued by large corporations
    d. dollar-denominated deposits at foreign banks or foreign branches of American banks
    e. short-term debt of the U.S. government
    f. an order to a bank by a customer to pay a sum of money at a future date

2. The price quotations of Treasury bonds in the <u>Wall Street Journal</u> show an ask price of 101:12 and a bid price of 101:07.
    a. As a buyer of the bond what is the dollar price you expect to pay?
    b. As a seller of the bond what is the dollar price you expect to receive?

3. Explain the chief characteristics of U.S. Treasury bills, notes, and bonds.

4. What is the major difference between commercial paper and asset-backed commercial paper?

5. Who issues municipal bonds? What is the difference between a general obligation bond, a revenue bond, and an industrial development bond?

6. An investor is considering the purchase of either a municipal or a corporate bond that pay before tax rates of return of 6.92% and 9.67%, respectively. If the investor is in the 25% marginal tax bracket, his or her after tax rates of return on the municipal and corporate bonds would be _____ and _____, respectively.

7. A 6.25% 25-year municipal bond is currently priced to yield 8.7%. For a taxpayer in the 25% marginal tax bracket, this bond would offer an equivalent taxable yield of _____.

8. In order for you to be indifferent between the after tax returns on a corporate bond paying 8.15% and a tax-exempt municipal bond paying 6.32%, what would your tax bracket need to be?

9. If three stocks comprise an index and the returns on the three stocks during a given period were 17%, -13%, and 6%, what would be the equally-weighted return of the index?

10. Compute the after-tax return to a corporation that buys a share of preferred stock at the beginning of the year for $65, receives a dividend of $4.50 during the year, and sells the stock at the end of the year for $65. The corporation is in the 30% tax bracket.

11. Suppose that your federal income tax rate is 33% and your state income tax rate is 4%.
    a. What is your approximate combined income tax rate?
    b. What is your exact combined income tax rate? Why is this less than the approximate rate?
    c. Confirm your calculation of the exact combined income tax rate by constructing an example for a person with $100 of taxable income.

    Answer questions 12 through 14 based on the information given in the following table.

Stock	Current Price	# of shares outstanding
Stock A	$35	2,000
Stock B	$82	4,500
Stock C	$21	1,600

12. The price-weighted index constructed with the three stocks is _____.

13. The value-weighted index constructed with the three stocks using a divisor of 1,000 is _____.

4

14. Assume that the returns on stocks A, B, and C for the year were 18%, -6%, and 30%, respectively. Assume that none of the stocks paid dividends and no stock splits occurred.
    a. The return of the price-weighted index would be _____.
    b. The return of the value-weighted index would be _____.
    c. The arithmetic return of the equally-weighted index would be _____.

15. Answer the questions below based on the information given in the following table. Stock C had a 2-1 split between time 0 and time 1.

	P_0	Q_0	P_1	Q_1
Stock A	$22	200	$22	200
Stock B	$15	400	$15	400
Stock C	$82	100	$41	200

    a. What is the value of a price-weighted index of the three stocks at time 0?
    b. What should be the value of a price-weighted index of the three stocks at time 1?
    c. What would the divisor of the price-weighted index be at time 1?
    d. What is the rate of return on a price-weighted index of the three stocks for the period (time 0 to time 1)?

16. a. What is a put option?
    b. What is a call option?
    c. What is a long position in a futures contract?
    d. What is a short position in a futures contract?

17. You purchased a futures contract on corn at a futures price of 350.25 and at the time of expiration the price was 362.25. What was your profit or loss? What would have been your profit if you would have been short the futures contract?

Chapter 3
How Securities Are Traded

1. Houndstooth, Inc. just sold 1,000,000 shares in a public offering at a price of $34 per share. The underwriting fee was 5.8% of the issue's total value based on the offering price. As soon as the shares were issued, the price jumped to $46 per share. What was the total cost of the issue? (Be sure to include both implicit and explicit costs.)

2. Complete the following items that describe the different types of markets.
   a. New securities are offered to the public through the _____ market.
   b. In a(n) _____ market, buyers and sellers meet in one place to buy or sell assets.
   c. In a(n) _____ market, the participants purchase assets for their own inventory, then sell them for a profit.
   d. Buyers and sellers must find each other on their own in a(n) _____ market.
   e. When a security trades after its original issue date, the trade takes place in a(n) _____ market.
   f. A(n) _____ market is one in which an agent provides search services to match buyers and sellers.

3. Fill in each of the following descriptions with the type of order it represents.
   a. A _____ order expires at the end of the trading day if it has not been executed.
   b. A _____ order gives the broker instructions to buy the stock if and when its price falls below a certain level.
   c. A _____ order tells the broker to buy or sell stock at current market prices.
   d. A _____ order instructs the broker to buy the stock if and when its price goes above a certain level.

4. a. You purchased Research in Motion (RIMM) for $79.83 per share. Its current price is $71.17. If the price goes below $70.00 per share you think it could be headed even lower. What kind of order would you call in to your broker to avoid bigger losses?
   b. Now suppose the current price of RIMM is $92.17. If the price goes to $94.00 you want to take the gain. What type of order would you place with your broker?

5. Assume you purchased 400 shares of IBM common stock on margin at $85 per share from your broker. If the initial margin is 60%, how much did you borrow from the broker?

6. You sold short 350 shares of common stock at $42 per share. The initial margin was 60%. Your initial investment was _____.

7. You purchased 1000 shares of Cisco common stock on margin at $18 per share. Assume the initial margin is 50% and the maintenance margin is 30%. Below what stock price level would you get a margin call? Assume the stock pays no dividend; ignore interest on margin.

8. You purchased 600 shares of common stock on margin at $27 per share. Assume the initial margin is 50% and the stock pays no dividend. What would the maintenance margin be if a margin call is made at a stock price of $22? Ignore interest on margin.

9. You purchased 200 shares of common stock on margin for $35 per share. The initial margin is 50% and the stock pays no dividend. What would your rate of return be if you sell the stock at $45.50 per share? Ignore interest on margin.

10. Assume you sell short 100 shares of common stock at $30 per share, with initial margin of 60%. What would be your rate of return if you repurchase the stock at $37/share? The stock paid no dividends during the period, and you did not remove any money from the account before making the offsetting transaction.

11. You sold short 200 shares of common stock at $50 per share. The initial margin is 50%. At what stock price would you receive a margin call if the maintenance margin is 35%?

12. Assume you sold short 100 shares of common stock at $25 per share. The initial margin is 50%. What would be the maintenance margin if a margin call is made at a stock price of $30?

13. You want to purchase AMAT stock at $42 from your broker using as little of your own money as possible. If initial margin is 50% and you have $2,700 to invest, how many shares can you buy?

14. You bought 150 shares of Citicorp for $25 per share, with an initial margin of 55%. The next day Citicorp's price drops to $20 per share. What is your actual margin?

15. What do the CFA Institute's Standards of Professional Conduct say about the following?
    a. receiving compensation in addition to that received from the employer
    b. priority of transactions for clients, employers and members
    c. the use of inside (nonpublic) information

16. What are circuit breakers? Why are circuit breaker used? Explain trading halts and collars.

17. What were the three broad practices that led to the financial scandals of 2000-2002 and what has been the regulatory response to those scandals?

Chapter 4
Mutual Funds and Other Investment Companies

1. a. What is an investment company?
   b. What are the four functions performed by investment companies?

2. A mutual fund had year-end assets of $750,000,000 and liabilities of $8,000,000. There were 40,750,000 shares in the fund at year end. What was the mutual fund's Net Asset Value?

3. A mutual fund had year-end assets of $316,000,000 and liabilities of $42,000,000. If the fund's NAV was $28.64, how many shares must have been held in the fund?

4. Compare unit investment trusts, open-end mutual funds, and closed-end mutual funds with regard to the items in the following table.

	Unit Investment Trust	Open-end Mutual Fund	Closed-end Mutual Fund
Management			
Type of Assets			
Fees			
# of Shares			
Purchase			
Redemption			

5. Fill in each of the following descriptions with the type of mutual fund classification it represents.
   a. A(n) _____ fund attempts to match the performance of a broad market index.
   b. A(n) _____ fund has a net asset value that is fixed at $1 per share and may offer a check-writing option.
   c. A(n) _____ fund holds both equities and fixed-income securities in fairly stable proportions.
   d. A(n) _____ fund holds primarily stock, but may also hold fixed-income or other types of securities.
   e. A(n) _____ fund holds both equities and fixed-income securities and varies the proportions to take advantage of forecasted market conditions.
   f. A(n) _____ fund holds securities of firms in a particular industry or sector.
   g. A(n) _____ fund primarily holds fixed-income securities.
   h. A(n) _____ fund is a balanced fund in which the mix of securities depends on the age of the investor.

6. Define the terms "front-end load" and "back-end load" as they are used in connection with open-end mutual funds.

7. A mutual fund had NAV per share of $14.25 on January 1, 2007. On December 31 of the same year the fund's NAV was $14.87. Income distributions were $0.59 and the fund had capital gain distributions of $1.36. Without considering taxes and transactions costs, what rate of return did an investor receive on the fund last year?

8. A mutual fund had NAV per share of $16.25 on January 1, 2007. On December 31 of the same year the fund's rate of return for the year was 14.2%. Income distributions were $1.02 and the fund had capital gain distributions of $0.63. Without considering taxes and transactions costs, what ending NAV would you calculate?

9. A mutual fund had average daily assets of $1.8 billion in 2007. The fund sold $625 million worth of stock and purchased $900 million worth of stock during the year. The fund's turnover ratio is _____.

10. You purchased shares of a mutual fund at a NAV of $18.00 per share at the beginning of the year and paid a front-end load of 5.75%. If the securities in which the fund invested increased in value by 12% during the year, and the fund's expense ratio was 0.75%, your return if you sold the fund at the end of the year would be _____.

11. Apex fund has a NAV of $16.12 and a front load of 5.62%. What is the offer price?

12. Exponential growth fund has an offer price of 14.77 and a load of 6%. What is the NAV?

13. A fund owns only three stocks with prices and quantities shown below. The fund has 50,000 shares outstanding. If the fund has $47,000 in liabilities, its NAV is

    _____.

Stock	Price	# of shares outstanding
Stock A	$35	2,000
Stock B	$82	4,500
Stock C	$21	1,600

14. You have decided to invest $10,000 in the Pinnacle fund. Over the long haul, the Pinnacle fund is expected to earn a return of 10.25% on the portfolio (gross of fees). However, Pinnacle fund offers several classes of funds. Therefore, you can choose to pay a front load of 5% and escape 12-b1 fees or you can avoid the load fee by paying 12-b1 fees of 0.75%. If your investment horizon is 16 years, which should you choose?

15. You have $5,000 to invest. The mutual fund you are considering offers two classes of shares. Class A shares have no front-end load, an expense ratio of 2%, and an expected gross return of 6.8% per year. Class B shares have a 5.5% front-end load, an expense ratio of 1.2%, and an expected gross return of 7.2% per year. Fill in the entries in the following table, and then indicate which of the classes you would prefer if you plan to hold the shares for four years. Which would you prefer if you plan to hold them for eight years?

	Class A	Class B
Initial Investment		
Value after 4 years		
Value after 8 years		

16. What does turnover measure and why is it important to mutual fund investors?

17. Suppose superfund had $88 million in average daily assets. Superfund sold $22 million in stock and purchased $44 million in different stock during the year. What is superfund's turnover?

Chapter 5
Learning about Return and Risk from the Historical Record

1. Over the past year you earned a nominal rate of interest of 9 % on your money. The inflation rate was 1.2 % over the same period. The exact actual growth rate of your purchasing power was _____.

2. A year ago, you invested $5,000 in a savings account that pays an annual interest rate of 3%. What is your approximate annual real rate of return if the rate of inflation was 1.5% over the year?

3. If the annual real rate of interest is 3% and the expected inflation rate is 2%, the nominal rate of interest would be approximately _____.

4. A year ago, you invested $5,000 in a savings account that pays an annual interest rate of 3.5%. What is your approximate after tax real rate of return if the rate of inflation was 2.5% over the year and your marginal tax bracket is 33%?

5. a. What effective annual rate (EAR) corresponds to a continuously compounded rate of 7.00%?
   b. If your bank pays interest at an effective annual rate (EAR) of 8.75%, what continuously compounded rate does the bank's competitor need to pay to offer an equally attractive investment?

6. You purchased a share of stock for $27. One year later you received $1.50 as dividend and sold the share for $28. What was your holding period return?

   Use the following information to answer questions 6 through 9. The probability distribution for the holding period return on Infospace stock is:

State of the Economy	Probability	HPR
Boom	.60	19%
Normal growth	.30	13%
Recession	.10	- 6%

7. What is the expected holding period return for Infospace stock?

8. What is the expected variance for Infospace stock?

9. What is the expected standard deviation for Infospace stock?

10. If the risk-free rate is 3%, what is the risk premium on Infospace stock?

11. AMAT stock has the following probability distribution of expected prices one year from now:

State	Probability	Price
1	25%	$55
2	40%	$62
3	35%	$71

   If you buy AMAT today for $50 and it will pay a dividend during the year of $3 per share, what is your expected holding period return on AMAT?

12. If the risk premium on AMAT stock is 29%, the risk-free rate must be _____.

13. You are the manager of the Innovative Ideas mutual fund. The following table reflects the activity of the fund during the last quarter. The fund started the quarter on January 1 with a balance of $100 million.

Innovative Ideas Mutual Fund
Monthly Returns

January	3.49%
February	2.24%
March	−2.17%
April	2.53%
May	4.48%
June	−0.04%

a. Calculate the arithmetic average return on the fund for the first half of the year.
b. Calculate the geometric (time-weighted) average return on the fund for the first half of the year.
c. What would be an unbiased estimate for the expected monthly return on the fund?
d. If you had invested $1,000 in the fund at the beginning of January, how much would you have in your account at the end of June?

14. Treetop Mutual fund has experienced an arithmetic average annual return of 10.95% and a geometric average return of 10.29% over the last five years. The standard deviation of the fund's returns is 8.49%. What is the Sharpe measure for the Treetop fund? Assume that the risk-free rate averaged 5.2% during the period.

15. Suppose you are examining an investment that has an expected return of 12.4% and a standard deviation of 30.6%. Calculate the upper and lower bounds for each of the following intervals, assuming that returns are normally distributed.
    a. an interval that would contain 68.26% of the expected outcomes
    b. an interval that would contain 95.44% of the expected outcomes
    c. an interval that would contain 99.74% of the expected outcomes

16. Your firm invested $2,500,000 in 270-day commercial paper today. At the end of the investment period (in 270 days) the firm will receive $2,585,000.
    a. What is the 270-day holding period rate of return on the investment?
    b. How many 270-day periods are there in one year? (Use a 365-day year.)
    c. What is the annual percentage rate APR earned on the investment?
    d. What is the effective annual rate (EAR)?
    e. Why is the EAR higher than the APR?

17. Because investors often assume that returns are normally, or approximately normally, distributed, it is useful to examine that assumption. Why would investors want to examine the assumption of normality? List and explain two tests that can be used to examine the normality assumption.

Chapter 6
Risk Aversion and Capital Allocation to Risky Assets

1. A portfolio has an expected rate of return of 14% and a standard deviation of 25%. The risk-free rate is 4 percent. An investor has the following utility function:

   $U = E(r) - .5(A)(\sigma^2)$. Which value of A makes this investor indifferent between the risky portfolio and the risk-free asset?

   Use the following information to answer questions 2 through 4.

Investment	Expected Return E(r)	Standard Deviation
A	0.12	0.29
B	0.15	0.35
C	0.24	0.38
D	0.29	0.44

   $$U = E(r) - (.5)(A)(\sigma^2), \text{ where } A = 3.0.$$

2. Based on the utility function above, which investment would you select?

3. Based on the previous table, which investment would you select if you were risk neutral?

4. Now suppose there is an investor with A = –2 rather than 3.0. Which investment would this person prefer? Why?

5. An investor can choose to invest in T-bills paying 4% or a risky portfolio with an end-of-year cash flow of $24,000. If the investor requires a risk premium of 7.5%, what would she be willing to pay for the risky portfolio?

6. An investment in Ukrainian Egg Decorators, Inc. has an expected return of 12.9% and a standard deviation of 18.6%.
   a. Calculate the utility level of this investment for three different investors: one with a risk aversion coefficient of $A_1 = 1.5$, a second with $A_2 = 3.5$, and a third with $A_3 = 6.0$. Use the utility function $U = E(r) - (.5)(A)(\sigma^2)$.
   b. What is the certainty equivalent rate of return for each of the investors? Explain the results.

7. What is the Mean-Variance criterion? Use the Mean-Variance criterion to determine which of the following investments are efficient and which are inefficient.

Investment	Expected Return	Standard Deviation of Returns
A	5.30%	9.30%
B	12.40%	11.40%
C	14.63%	8.47%
D	37.47%	9.40%
E	7.90%	47.20%
F	3.83%	1.25%

8. Which of the investments in the graph below is clearly preferred to investment Q for any risk averse investor? Which investments could potentially be on the same indifference curve as Q fir a given investor?

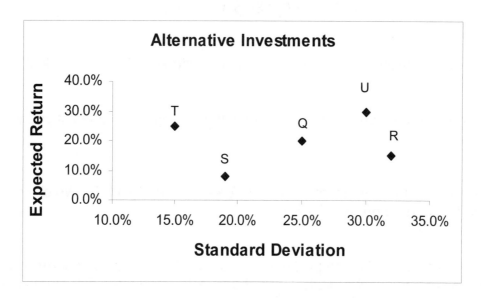

9. An investor invests 70 percent of his wealth in a risky asset with an expected rate of return of 12% and a variance of 0.04 and 30 percent in a T-bill that pays 5%. His portfolio's expected return and standard deviation are _____ and _____ respectively.

Refer to the following information in answering questions 10 through 17.

You plan to invest $100 in a risky asset with an expected rate of return of 13% and a standard deviation of 14% and a T-bill with a rate of return of 4%.

10. What percentages of your money must be invested in the risky asset and the risk-free asset, respectively, to form a portfolio with an expected return of 8%?

11. What would the standard deviation of the portfolio formed in the previous question be?

12. What percentages of your money must be invested in the risk-free asset and the risky asset, respectively, to form a portfolio with a standard deviation of 5%?

13. Given the initial investment of $100, a portfolio that has an expected outcome of $122 is formed by _____.

14. a. What is the slope of the Capital Allocation Line (CAL) formed with the risky asset and the risk-free asset?
    b. What is the intercept of the CAL?
    c. What is the equation for the CAL?

15. Now suppose that the investor may still lend at a risk-free rate of 4%, but if she needs to borrow, she will have to pay 9%. Draw a picture of the new CAL. What is the slope of the CAL over the segment that corresponds to borrowing?

16. If she decides to borrow $30 to add to her $100 investment in the risky asset, her expected return of the portfolio should be _____.

17. If she decides to borrow $30 to add to her $100 investment in the risky asset, her expected standard deviation of the portfolio should be _____.

Chapter 7
Optimal Risky Portfolios

Refer to the following information to answer questions 1 through 9 below.

Consider the following probability distribution for stocks K and L:

State	Probability	Return on Stock K	Return on Stock L
1	0.10	10%	9%
2	0.20	11%	8%
3	0.40	12%	7%
4	0.20	13%	6%
5	0.10	14%	9%

1. The expected rates of return of stocks K and L are _____ and _____ respectively.

2. The standard deviations of stocks K and L are _____ and _____, respectively.

3. The covariance between stocks K and L is _____.

4. The coefficient of correlation between stocks K and L is _____.

5. If you invest 35% of your money in K and 65% in L, what will be your portfolio's expected rate of return?

6. If you invest 35% of your money in K and 65% in L, what will be your portfolio's expected return and standard deviation?

7. Let G be the global minimum variance portfolio. The weights of K and L in G are _____ and _____, respectively.

8. The expected rate of return of the global minimum variance portfolio, G, is _____.

9. The expected standard deviation of the global minimum variance portfolio, G, is _____.

10. Security A has expected return of 11% and standard deviation of 22%. Security B has expected return of 16% and standard deviation of 29%. If the two securities have a correlation coefficient of 0.6, what is their covariance?

11. a. Given an optimal risky portfolio with expected return of 11% and standard deviation of 20% and a risk free rate of 4%, what is the slope of the best feasible CAL?
    b. Draw a graph of the CAL. (Hint: Plot the risk-free asset and the optimal risky portfolio, then join them with a straight line to get the CAL.) Show the optimal risky portfolio's position in the CAL; label this point P.
    c. Now suppose you want to form a complete portfolio by investing 80% of your funds in portfolio P and the rest in the risk-free asset. Show the approximate position of your complete portfolio on the CAL; label this point C.

Use the following information to answer questions 12 through 15.

T-bills currently offer a return of 4.90%. You have constructed an optimal portfolio of risky assets (portfolio O) by putting 23% of your investment in Mutual Fund A and 77% in Mutual Fund B. Fund A has an expected return of 8% and Fund B has an expected return of 19%.

12. What is the expected return on portfolio O?

13. Suppose that you have decided to create a complete portfolio (portfolio C) by putting 34% of your funds in the risk-free asset and the remainder in portfolio O. What is the expected return on the complete portfolio?

14. If portfolio O's standard deviation is 21%, what is the standard deviation of the complete portfolio?

15. Determine the weights of the risk-free asset, Fund A, and Fund B in the complete portfolio.

Refer to the following information to answer questions 16 through 18 below.

Consider the following returns, standard deviations, and correlations for stocks 1 through 4.

Stock	Weight	Return	Standard Deviation
1	0.10	10%	16%
2	0.20	11%	17%
3	0.40	12%	18%
4	0.20	13%	19%

Correlation Matrix

	1	2	3	4
1	1			
2	0.20	1		
3	0.40	0.60	1	
4	0.30	0.70	0.50	1

16. The return of the portfolio would be _____.

17. The variance of the portfolio would be _____.

18. The standard deviation of the portfolio would be _____.

Chapter 8
Index Models

1. Assume that stock market returns do not resemble a single-index structure. An investment fund analyzes 450 stocks in order to construct a mean-variance efficient portfolio constrained by 450 investments. They will need to calculate _____ expected returns and _____ variances of returns.

2. Assume that stock market returns do not resemble a single-index structure. An investment fund analyzes 450 stocks in order to construct a mean-variance efficient portfolio constrained by 450 investments. They will need to calculate _____ covariances.

3. Assume that stock market returns do follow a single-index structure. An investment fund analyzes 250 stocks in order to construct a mean-variance efficient portfolio constrained by 250 investments. They will need to calculate _____ estimates of expected excess returns and _____ estimates of sensitivity coefficients to the common macroeconomic factor.

4. Consider the single-index model. The alpha of a stock is 0%. The return on the market index is 12%. The risk-free rate of return is 5%. The stock earns a return that exceeds the risk-free rate by 7% and there are no firm-specific events affecting the stock performance. The β of the stock is _____.

5. Suppose you held a well-diversified portfolio with a very large number of securities, and that the single index model holds. If the standard deviation of your portfolio was 0.22 and the standard deviation of the market was 0.18, the β of the portfolio would be approximately _____.

6. The index model has been estimated from the excess returns for stock A with the following results:

$$R_A = 0.12 + 0.9R_M + e_A \qquad \sigma_M = 0.24 \qquad \sigma(e_A) = 0.12$$

The standard deviation of the return for stock A is _____.

Use the following information to answer questions 7 through 11.

The index model has been estimated for stocks A and B with the following results:

$$R_A = 0.12 + 0.6R_M + e_A \qquad R_B = 0.04 + 1.4R_M + e_B$$

$$\sigma_M = 0.26 \qquad \sigma(e_A) = 0.20 \qquad \sigma(e_B) = 0.10$$

7. What is the covariance between the returns on stocks A and B?

8. What is the variance of each stock?

9. Break down the variance of each stock into the systematic risk and the firm-specific risk components.

10. What is the covariance between each stock and the market index?

11. What is the correlation coefficient between the two stocks?

12. The beta of Exxon Mobile Corp. (XOM) stock has been estimated as 1.43 using regression analysis on a sample of historical returns. The Merrill Lynch adjusted beta of XOM stock would be _____.

13. Suppose the equation $\beta_t = 0.4 + 0.85\,\beta_{t-1}$ best describes the evolution of β over time. If a stock had a β of 0.8 last year, you would forecast the β to be _____ in the coming year.

14. You expect the market index to earn a return of 12% in the coming year. Treasury bills are yielding 5%. The unadjusted β of Deutsche Telekom AG (DT) stock is 1.25. If you use Merrill Lynch adjusted betas, what is a reasonable forecast of the return on DT stock for the coming year?

15. The following model has been estimated for use in forecasting beta: forecast beta = .047 + 0.88(current beta) + 6.3(growth in earnings per share) – 0.4(debt ratio). What would you forecast beta to be for a firm that has a current beta of 1.24, expected growth of .053 in earnings per share, and a debt ratio of 0.74?

16. When security returns can be well approximated by normal distributions that are correlated across securities, it is said that the securities are _____. This assumption alone implies that, at any one time, _____. When more than one variable drives normally distributed security returns, these returns are said to have a _____ distribution.

17. The optimal portfolio derived from the single-index model can be inferior to the full (Markowitz) covariance model when stocks with correlated residuals have _____ and account for _____ of the portfolio. If many pairs of the stocks exhibit residual correlation, it is possible that a _____ would be better suited to portfolio construction and _____.

Chapter 9
The Capital Asset Pricing Model

1. a. The risk-free rate is 3.9% and the standard deviation of the market portfolio is 17.0%. If the average investor has a risk aversion coefficient of 1.7, what is the equilibrium value of the market risk premium? What is the expected rate of return on the market?
   b. Recalculate your answers to part a if the average investor has a risk aversion coefficient equal to 2.8. Why do your answers make sense?

2. The risk-free rate and the expected market rate of return are 3.5% and 10.5%, respectively. According to the capital asset pricing model (CAPM), the expected rate of return on a security with a beta of 1.63 is equal to _____.

3. Your personal opinion is that IBM has an expected rate of return of 12%. It has a beta of 1.25. The risk-free rate is 3.5% and the market expected rate of return is 10.5%. According to the Capital Asset Pricing Model, is IBM under priced, overpriced, or fairly priced?

4. You invest $550 in a security with a beta of 1.12 and $450 in a security with a beta of 0.86. The beta of the resulting portfolio is _____.

5. Security A has an expected rate of return of 11% and a beta of 1.1. The market expected rate of return is 7.5% and the risk-free rate is 4.5%. The alpha of the stock is _____.

6. Given the following two stocks A and B

Security	Expected rate of return	Beta
A	12.2%	1.23
B	13.9%	1.81

   If the expected market rate of return is 10.5% and the risk-free rate is 3.5%, which security would be considered the better buy and why?

7. Assume that a security is fairly priced and has an expected rate of return of 15%. The market expected rate of return is 10.5% and the risk-free rate is 3.5%. The beta of the stock is ___?

8. A security has an expected rate of return of 13% and a beta of 1.1. The risk-free rate is 3.5%. If you consider the stock to be fairly priced, the market expected rate of return must be _____ .

9. A security has an expected rate of return of 12% and a beta of 1.27. The market expected rate of return is 10.5%. If you consider the stock to be fairly priced, the risk-free rate must be _____ .

10. If the variance of the market is .05 and the covariance of GM with the market is 0.06, the beta of GM stock must be _____ .

11. A stock has a beta of 0.86 and a covariance with the market of 0.05. The variance of the market must be _____ .

12. The return on the risk-free asset is 4%. The expected return on the market portfolio is 11%.
    a. What is the intercept of the Security Market Line (SML)?
    b. What is the slope of the SML?
    c. What is the expected return on asset E, which has a beta of 1.37?
    d. Draw the SML. Use the label "M" to show the point that represents the market portfolio and the label "E" to show the point that represents asset E.

13. The common stock of Long Beach Ladder Company has a beta of 1.7. The firm is considering the purchase of additional capital equipment so it can take on a project that will update the plant and expand its production capacity. The project is riskier than the firm's existing operations and has a beta of 2.0. The risk-free rate is 5% and the expected return on the market is 12%. What discount rate should the firm use to evaluate the project? The project's cash flows are shown in the table below. Find the net present value of the project. Should Long Beach Ladder take on the project?

Time	Cash Flow
0	–$175,000
1	$57,000
2	$57,000
3	$57,000
4	$57,000
5	$57,000

14. You estimate that the risk-free rate of return is 6.1% and the expected return on the market portfolio is 14.6%.
    a. Use the CAPM to calculate the expected returns on Stocks 1 through 4 based on the information in the table below.
    b. Draw a graph of the SML.
    c. Show the position of each asset relative to the SML.
    d. Indicate whether each asset is underpriced, overpriced, or correctly priced and calculate its alpha.

	Stock 1	Stock 2	Stock 3	Stock 4
B_i	−0.10	0.67	1.95	2.20
CAPM $E(r_i)$				
Actual $E(r_i)$	6.29%	9.08%	27.24%	24.80%
Fairly Priced?				
$alpha_i$				

15. You are thinking of investing in a stock that pays a perpetual dividend of $6.00. Based on your research, you believe that the stock has a beta coefficient of 0.90. The current risk-free rate of return is 4.30% and the expected return on the market is 13%.
    a. What expected return would you require on this stock based on your estimates?
    b. Given this expected return, what would you be willing to pay for this stock?
    c. Suppose that you made a mistake in your research and the actual beta of the stock is 1.30. Would you have overpaid or underpaid for the stock if you bought it for the price you found in part b?

16. Briefly explain the simplifying assumptions that lead to the basic version of CAPM.

17. Briefly summarize the Consumption CAPM (CCAPM) and why it is important.

Chapter 10
Arbitrage Pricing Theory and
Multifactor Models of Risk and Return

1. a. What is arbitrage?
   b. What is a zero-investment portfolio?
   c. How are these two concepts used in Arbitrage Pricing Theory (APT)?
   d. What are the coefficients on the APT factors called?

2. Consider a single factor APT. Portfolio A has a beta of 1.2 and an expected return of 14%. Portfolio B has a beta of 0.7 and an expected return of 9%. The risk-free rate of return is 5%. If you wanted to take advantage of an arbitrage opportunity, you should take a short position in portfolio _____ and a long position in portfolio _____.

3. Consider the one-factor APT. The variance of returns on the factor portfolio is .05. The beta of a well-diversified portfolio on the factor is 1.3. The variance of returns on the well-diversified portfolio is approximately _____.

4. Consider the one-factor APT. The standard deviation of returns on a well-diversified portfolio is 20%. The standard deviation on the factor portfolio is 17%. The beta of the well-diversified portfolio is approximately _____.

5. Consider the single-factor APT. Stocks A and B have expected returns of 12% and 16%, respectively. The risk-free rate of return is 5%. Stock B has a beta of 1.1. If arbitrage opportunities are ruled out, stock A has a beta of _____.

6. Consider the multifactor APT with two factors. Stock A has an expected return of 12.2%, a beta of 1.2 on factor 1 and a beta of .6 on factor 2. The risk premium on the factor 1 portfolio is 4%. The risk-free rate of return is 5%. What is the risk-premium on factor 2 if no arbitrage opportunities exist?

7. Consider the multifactor model APT with two factors. Portfolio A has a beta of 0.92 on factor 1 and a beta of 1.37 on factor 2. The risk premiums on the factor 1 and factor 2 portfolios are 2.3% and 3.4%, respectively. The risk-free rate of return is 4%. The expected return on portfolio A is _____ if no arbitrage opportunities exist.

8. Consider the multifactor APT with two factors. The risk premiums on the factor 1 and factor 2 portfolios are 5% and 6%, respectively. Stock A has a beta of 1.0 on factor 1, and a beta of 0.9 on factor 2. The expected return on stock A is 15%. If no arbitrage opportunities exist, the risk-free rate of return is _____.

9. Consider the multifactor APT. The risk premiums on the factor 1 and factor 2 portfolios are 3% and 4%, respectively. The risk-free rate of return is 6%. Stock A has an expected return of 14% and a beta on factor 1 of 0.8. Stock A has a beta on factor 2 of _____.

10. Assume that there are three stocks, A, B, and C and that you can either invest in these stocks or short sell them. There are also three possible states of nature for economic growth in the upcoming year (strong, moderate, or weak). The returns for the upcoming year on stocks A, B, and C for each of these states of nature are given below:

| | State of Nature | | |
Stock	Strong Growth	Moderate Growth	Weak Growth
A	37%	18%	−8%
B	31%	12%	−4%
C	33%	16%	−6%

If you invested in an equally weighted portfolio of stocks A and C, your portfolio return would be _____ if economic growth were moderate.

11. In the APT model, what is the nonsystematic standard deviation of an equally-weighted, well diversified portfolio of 60 securities that has an average value (across securities) of nonsystematic standard deviation, $\sigma(e_i)$, equal to 22%?

12. Suppose that well-diversified portfolio Z is priced based on two factors. The beta for the first factor is 1.10 and the beta for the second factor is 0.45. The expected return on the first factor is 11%. The expected return on the second factor is 17%. The risk-free rate of return is 5.2%. Use the arbitrage pricing theory relationships to answer the following questions.
   a. What is the risk premium on the first factor?
   b. What is the risk premium on the second factor?
   c. What is the risk premium on portfolio Z due to its exposure to the first factor?
   d. What is the risk premium on portfolio Z due to its exposure to the second factor?
   e. What is the total risk premium on portfolio Z?
   f. What is the total expected return on portfolio Z?

13. What factors did Chen, Roll, and Ross suggest for use in the APT model?

14. What factors did Fama and French use in their model?

15. Assume that you are using a two-factor APT model to find the expected return on a stock. The factors, their betas, and their assumed risk premiums are shown in the table below. The risk-free rate is 4.8%.

Factor	Factor Beta	Assumed Factor Risk Premium
A	1.7	2.0%
B	0.9	10.5%

   a. What is the expected return on the stock if it is fairly priced?
   b. Now suppose that the factor risk premiums you used are found to be incorrect. The true factor risk premiums are shown below. Recalculate the expected return on the stock based on the true factor risk premiums.
   c. Compare your answers from parts a and b. If you based the expected return on the assumed factor risk premiums rather than the true ones, would you have overpriced or underpriced the stock?

Factor	Factor Beta	True Factor Risk Premium
A	1.7	3.5%
B	0.9	9.0%

16. What are the three key propositions underlying Ross's APT?

17. You can distinguish a multi-factor CAPM model from a multi-factor by examining because _____ risk factors will be inherited from sources of risk that a broad group of investors considers important enough to hedge. However, _____ is silent on where to look for priced risk factors.

Chapter 11
The Efficient Market Hypothesis

1. What does it mean to say that stock prices follow a random walk or submartingale?

2. What is technical analysis?

3. What is fundamental analysis?

4. What is the weak form of the EMH and what are the implications for security analysis?

5. What is the semistrong form of the EMH and what are the implications for security analysis?

6. What is the strong form of the EMH and what are the implications for security analysis?

7. What does it mean to state that the types of efficiency are cumulative?

8. Why do proponents of the EMH and proponents of technical analysis have opposing points of view?

9. Why does investing in mutual funds and exchange traded funds (ETFs) make sense for small investors?

10. Which market is likely to be more efficient – the market for Google stock or the market for the stock of a firm in an emerging market? Why?

11. Explain what an anomaly is and describe some anomalies that have been documented in security returns.

12. Describe the meanings of the magnitude issue, the selection bias issue, and the lucky event issue as they relate to the EMH.

13. Jonathan Corporation has a beta of 1.4. The annualized market return yesterday was 11%, and the risk-free rate is currently 5%. You observe that Jonathan had an annualized return yesterday of 16%. Assuming that markets are efficient, what would this suggest?

14. AMS Corporation announced yesterday that their same store sales increased by 3% over the same period last year. AMS has a beta of 1.6. The annualized market return was 12% yesterday, and the risk-free rate is currently 4%. You observe that AMS had an annualized return yesterday of 14%. Assuming that markets are efficient, what would this suggest?

15. Energy Corporation announced yesterday that they would enter into an international joint venture. Energy has a beta of 0.7. The annualized market return has been 10.5% for the past several weeks, and the risk-free rate has been 3.5% over the same period. You observe that Energy had an annualized return the day before yesterday of 12% and a return yesterday of 8.4%. What might this suggest?

16. Studies of the stock price response to dividend announcements by Patel and Wolfson (1984) reveal that stock prices react _____. Moreover, Busse and Green's (2002) research suggests that the stock price of firms mentioned on CNBC's "Morining" or "Midday Call" segments react to positive news within _____ and react to negative news within _____. This evidence _____ the contention that stock prices react quickly to news.

17. Studies of the earnings announcements reveal that firms with positive earnings surprises _____ while firms with negative earnings _____. In both cases, there is _____ reaction to the news. However, the reaction _____. Firms with positive surprises _____ while firms with negative surprises _____.

Chapter 12
Behavioral Finance and Technical Analysis

1. What is behavioral finance and what are the information processing errors and behavioral biases that have been documented?

2. Why does a belief in technical analysis conflict with a belief in the efficient markets hypothesis (EMH)?

3. Henry lost his job four months ago and has been able to find only low-wage jobs since then. As a result he is two months behind on his mortgage payments and has received notice that the bank may seize his house if he doesn't reconcile the issue within 10 days. He has almost no money in his regular savings account. However, he has a mutual fund with a substantial balance that is earmarked to fund his children's college educations. Henry is adamant that he will not invade these funds to solve his current dilemma.
   What behavioral characteristic is Henry exhibiting? Explain to Henry how this view is complicating his situation unnecessarily

4. Aunt Alma has held Green Grocer stock for 37 years. During most of that time she realized a steady increase of dividends at a growth rate of 2% per year. However, the past two years have been challenging for the company due to irregular weather patterns. As a result, there were no dividend increases during that time. Aunt Alma is now panicked because she believes she will not get the increase in dividends that she had been counting on in retirement. What behavioral characteristic is she exhibiting?

5. You are socializing with your colleagues when the subject of investing arises. Ed tells the group about his amazing success, saying that he has realized an 18% return in the last two months. The market was down 3% during that period. Other group members start to ask for his advice on what securities to buy and he names several possibilities. What behavioral qualities is Ed demonstrating and why might they cause problems for people who follow his advice?

6. How does the utility function hypothesized by prospect theory differ from a conventional utility function? What are the implications for investors if their utility functions are as described by prospect theory?

7. You are evaluating a closed-end mutual fund and see that its price is different from its net asset value (NAV). The fund has an expense ratio (ε) of 2.8% and a dividend yield (δ) of 4%. The fund has experienced a risk-adjusted abnormal return (α) of 2%. By what amount (premium or discount) is the fund likely to trade relative to its NAV? What would explain the discrepancy between the price and the NAV?

8. Round Barn stock has a required return of 11% and is expected to pay a dividend of $3.25 next year. Investors expect a growth rate of 6% on the dividends for the foreseeable future. What is the current fair price for the stock? Suppose the stock is selling at this price, but then investors revise their expectations. The new expectation for the growth rate is 5.20%. If investors are rational, what will be the new price for Round Barn stock?

9. What is the Dow theory? What are some of its variations?

10. How is the breadth of the market measured? How do financial analysts use market breadth as a measure of market trends?

11. Use the information in the table below to calculate the trin ratio for October 1 and February 1. State whether each ratio represents a bullish or a bearish outlook.

	October 1	February 1
Advances	8,511	8,785
Declines	4,214	10,861
Volume Advancing	2,441,578	3,517,846
Volume Declining	1,840,742	845,622

12. What is the confidence index? How does it work and how is it calculated?

13. On April 1 there are 202 put options and 259 call options outstanding on a stock. Calculate the put/call ratio and interpret your answer.

14. What is data mining? Why is it not very useful?

15. Draw a graph that shows the weekly closing prices for Rustic Relics based on the data in the table below. Calculate the 4-week moving average for these data and plot it on the same graph. Indicate buy and sell signals on the graph. If you had followed the buy and sell signals, would it have been a profitable strategy? Would considering transactions costs change your answer?

Date	Open	High	Low	Close
2-Mar-07	26.37	26.67	24.76	26.37
9-Mar-07	26.37	26.93	23.90	25.43
16-Mar-07	26.12	27.45	25.98	26.32
23-Mar-07	26.32	26.77	23.80	24.23
30-Mar-07	24.35	24.55	22.33	24.53
6-Apr-07	24.69	24.69	21.88	22.53
13-Apr-07	22.23	24.30	21.44	21.65
20-Apr-07	21.74	22.12	19.62	20.90
27-Apr-07	21.93	23.42	19.47	20.19
4-May-07	20.39	20.85	19.25	20.31
11-May-07	19.94	20.23	17.99	19.39
18-May-07	19.46	21.42	19.39	20.93
25-May-07	20.93	21.62	20.23	20.88
1-Jun-07	20.43	21.13	19.85	20.83
8-Jun-07	20.85	21.42	17.71	17.85
15-Jun-07	17.74	17.97	13.77	15.00
22-Jun-07	15.08	15.92	13.17	13.34
29-Jun-07	12.96	14.23	11.41	11.87
6-Jul-07	11.87	12.70	9.73	12.70
13-Jul-07	12.60	14.28	10.42	10.96
20-Jul-07	10.68	12.40	10.61	11.51
27-Jul-07	11.51	12.63	11.25	12.63
3-Aug-07	13.38	15.41	12.81	14.07
10-Aug-07	14.03	15.50	13.65	15.00
17-Aug-07	14.95	17.82	14.23	17.31
24-Aug-07	17.32	20.75	16.80	20.62

16. The Law of one Price should be satisfied in rational markets. List some examples of violations to the Law of One Price for financial assets.

17. Explain under what condition behavioral biases matter for stock pricing.

Chapter 13
Empirical Evidence on Security Returns

1. Explain the expected return-beta relationship.

2. What three steps did early simple tests of the CAPM follow?

3. How is the security characteristic line (SCL) estimated?

4. How is the security market line (SML) estimated?

5. What do the results of early tests of the CAPM by Lintner (1965) and Miller and Scholes (1972) show?

6. What conclusions have been drawn from the tests of the CAPM?

7. Why did Roll claim that the CAPM is not testable?

8. Why might the problems with early tests of the CAPM have been caused by measurement error?

9. How did Mayers' (1972) version of the CAPM compensate for the violation of the model's assumption that all assets are traded and accessible to all investors?

10. Why did Heaton and Lucas (2000) investigate the impact of non-traded businesses on investors' portfolios? Summarize the results of their study.

11. What multi-factor model did Chen, Roll, and Ross use to attempt to explain security returns?

12. What is the Fama-French three-factor model?

13. How did Davis, Fama, and French (2000) measure the small minus big (SMB) variable and the high minus low variable (HML) in their study?

14. What did Petkova and Zhang (2005) conclude about the relationship between beta and the market risk premium?

15. What is survivorship bias and how does it affect studies of performance in the mutual fund industry?

16. Early tests of the Consumption CAPM (CCAPM) found that CCAPM _____ the traditional CAPM. One challenge faced by early tests was that they used _____.

17. How did Jagannathan and Wang (2006) do to test the CCAPM and what were their major findings?

Chapter 14
Bond Prices and Yields

1. A Treasury bond due in one year has a yield of 4.7% and a Treasury bond due in 5 years has a yield of 5.7%. A bond issued by Microsoft due in 5 years has a yield of 7.9% and a bond issued by California Pizza Kitchen due in one year has a yield of 6.7%. The default risk premiums on the bonds issued by California Pizza Kitchen and Microsoft, respectively, are _____ and _____.

2. You have invested in a Treasury Inflation Protected Security (TIPS) that has a par value of $1,000 and a coupon rate of 4.6%. You paid par value for the security and it matures in two years. Assume that the inflation rate for next year is 3.2% and for the year after is 2.1%. Complete the following table by calculating the par values, the coupon payments, the principal repayment, the total payments and the nominal and real rates of return for the next two years.

Time	Inflation in Year Just Ended	Par Value	Coupon Payment	Principal Repayment	Total Payment	Nominal Return	Real Return
0		$1,000.00					
1	3.2%						
2	2.1%						

3. A coupon bond that pays interest annually has a par value of $1,000, matures in 6 years, and has a yield to maturity of 9.43%. The intrinsic value of the bond today will be _____ if the coupon rate is 7.25%.

4. A coupon bond that pays interest semi-annually has a par value of $1,000, matures in 5 years, and has a yield to maturity of 10%. The intrinsic value of the bond today will be _____ if the coupon rate is 11%.

5. A coupon bond that pays interest of $100 annually has a par value of $1,000, matures in 5 years, and is selling today at a $111 discount from par value. The yield to maturity on this bond is _____.

6. A coupon bond pays annual interest, has a par value of $1,000, matures in 8 years, has a coupon rate of 9%, and has a yield to maturity of 10.5%. The current yield on this bond is _____.

7. A zero-coupon bond has a yield to maturity of 9% and a par value of $1,000. If the bond matures in 4 years, the bond should sell for a price of _____ today.

8. You have just purchased a 12-year zero-coupon bond with a yield to maturity of 11% and a par value of $1,000. What would your rate of return at the end of the year be if you sell the bond? Assume the yield to maturity on the bond is 12% at the time you sell and ignore taxes.

9. A coupon bond is reported as having an ask price of 108 (that is, 108% of the $1,000 par value) in the Wall Street Journal. If the last interest payment was made two months ago and the coupon rate is 12%, the invoice price of the bond will be _____.

10. A Treasury bill with a par value of $10,000 due one month from now is selling today for $9,900. The effective annual yield is _____.

11. A convertible bond has a par value of $1,000 and a current market price of $995. The current price of the issuing firm's stock is $32 and the conversion ratio is 31 shares. The bond's market conversion value is _____.

12. A convertible bond has a par value of $1,000 and a current market value of $995. The current price of the issuing firm's stock is $32 and the conversion ratio is 31 shares. The bond's conversion premium is _____.

13. A 10% coupon bond ($1,000 par) that makes semiannual payments matures in 15 years. The bond is callable in 5 years at a call price of $1,070. If the bond is selling today for $1,100, the yield to call is _____.

14. A three-year bond with a par value of $1,000 is selling for $973. The bond has a coupon rate of 8% and makes interest payments annually. Suppose that the one-year interest rates over the next three years turn out to be 9% (from time 0 to time 1), 7% (from time 1 to time 2), and 10% (from time 2 to time 3). What would be the realized compound return on the bond?

15. You purchased an annual interest coupon bond one year ago with 8 years remaining to maturity at the time of purchase. The coupon interest rate is 10% and par value is $1,000. At the time you purchased the bond, the yield to maturity was 9%. If you sold the bond after receiving the first interest payment and the bond's yield to maturity had changed to 8%, your holding period return on the would have been _____. (Ignore taxes.)

16. A bond with a coupon rate of 5.40% is priced with an 8.00% yield to maturity. Coupon interest is paid semiannually. The bond has 4 years remaining until maturity. Assuming that market rates stay the same over the next 4 years, calculate the value of the bond for each year and the amount of change in the bond's value from year to year. Describe the behavior of the bond's value over time.

17. Why is preferred stock sometimes called a "hybrid" security? Relate your answer to a discussion of the main features of preferred stock, including the standing of preferred stockholders in bankruptcy, the dividends, and voting rights.

18. What are CDOs and how are they created?

19. How did CDO cause such an uproar in 2007?

Chapter 15
The Term Structure of Interest Rates

Refer to the following table to answer questions 1 through 5. Suppose that investors expect that interest rates for the next 4 years will be as follows:

Maturity (Years)	Yield to Maturity
1	4%
2	5%
3	6%
4	8%

1. What is the price of a 2-year zero-coupon bond with a par value of $1,000?

2. What is the price of a 3-year zero-coupon bond with a par value of $1,000?

3. What is the price of a 4-year zero-coupon bond with a par value of $1,000?

4. What is the price of a $1,000 par value bond with a 4-year maturity and a 10% coupon rate paid annually?

5. What is the yield to maturity of the 4-year coupon bond?

Refer to the following table to answer questions 6 through 11. The following is a list of prices for zero-coupon bonds with different maturities and par value of $1,000.

Maturity (Years)	Price
1	$952.38
2	$898.47
3	$831.92
4	$763.23

6. What is the yield to maturity on a 2-year zero-coupon bond?

7. What is the yield to maturity on a 3-year zero-coupon bond?

8. According to the expectations theory, what is the expected forward rate in the third year?

9. What is the price of a $1,000 par value bond with 4-years to maturity and a 12% coupon rate paid annually?

10. Calculate the forward rates for periods 2, 3, and 4.

11. You have purchased a 4-year maturity bond with a 10% coupon rate paid annually. The bond has a par value of $1,000. What would the price of the bond be one year from now if the implied forward rates stay the same?

12. If the yield on a 3-year zero-coupon bond is 6.8% and forward rates of 5.9% in year 1 and 6.6% in year 2, what must be the forward rate in year 3?

13. The yield to maturity on 1 year --coupon bonds is 6.3%. The yield to maturity on 2-year zero-coupon bonds is 7.9%.
    a. What is the forward rate of interest for the second year?
    b. According to the expectations hypothesis, what is the expected value of the one-year interest rate for next year?
    c. According to the liquidity preference theory, is the expected value of the one-year interest rate for next year higher or lower than the rate you found in part b?

14. Plot the pure yield curve implied by the data in the following table, which apply to zero-coupon Treasury issues.

Time to Maturity	Yield to Maturity
3 months	3.70%
6 months	3.90%
1 year	4.20%
2 years	5.20%
5 years	6.00%
10 years	5.70%
15 years	7.10%
20 years	6.29%

Based on the Expectations Hypothesis, what does the yield curve tell us about short-term interest rates 5 years from now? What does it tell us about short-term rates 15 years from now and 20 years from now?

15. How are a pure yield curve and an on-the-run yield curve similar and how are they different?

16. What are Treasury STRIPS and what is the relationship between bond stripping, bond reconstitution, arbitrage, and the Law of One Price?

17. Assume that you were reading the bond quotations and noticed that the price of a Treasury bond was more than the price of the STRIPS required to reconstitute the bond. What action would take to profit from this observation? What would likely happen to the price of similar Treasury bonds and STRIPS?

Chapter 16
Managing Bond Portfolios

1. What is duration and why is it important in fixed-income portfolio management?

2. What is convexity and why is it important in fixed-income portfolio management?

3. A five-year par value bond with a coupon rate of 8% (with annual payments) has a duration of _____ and a modified duration of _____.

4. Bond XYZ is selling at par and has a modified duration of 8.32. If the market yield increases by 1% the bond's price will _____ by _____.

5. Which of the following bonds has the longest duration?
   a. a 5-year maturity, 0% coupon bond.
   b. a 5-year maturity, 8% coupon bond.
   c. a 15-year maturity, 8% coupon bond.
   d. a 15-year maturity, 0% coupon bond.

6. Calculate the prices of the bonds described below, which pay annual coupon interest. Assuming that 6.4% is the current yield to maturity, calculate the percentage change in price that would result from the yield changes shown. What do your answers confirm regarding the interest rate sensitivity of bonds?

Par	$1,000	$1,000	$1,000
Coupon Rate	6%	6%	6%
Years to Maturity	12	12	12
Yield	5.90%	**6.40%**	6.90%

7. If the required yield is 9%, what is the duration of perpetuity that pays $2,500 annually?

8. A corporate bond was recently selling to yield 10%. The Macaulay duration for the bond is 12.45 years. Given this information, the bond's modified duration would be _____.

9. A bond has a yield to maturity of 8.5% and duration of 5.25 years. If the market yield falls by 31 basis points, what percentage change will there be in the bond's price?

10. Consider a bond selling at par with modified duration of 14.2 years and convexity of 185. A 1% decrease in yield would cause the price to increase by 14.2%, according to the duration rule. What would be the percentage price change according to the duration-with-convexity rule?

11. What are the two types of risk fixed-income investors face? Explain why these two types of risk are offsetting, which allows for immunization of the fixed-income position.

12. Your firm has an obligation to pay out $60,000 in 3 years and $190,000 in 8 years. You want to immunize this liability with zero-coupon bonds that have a maturity of 2 years and a perpetuity that makes annual payments. The current market interest rate is 7.00%.
    a. Calculate the duration of the liability.
    b. What is the duration of the zero-coupon bond? What is the duration of the perpetuity?
    c. What proportions of your investment should you put into the zero-coupon bond and into the perpetuity to immunize your position?
    d. How much, in dollars, should you invest in each of the assets?
    e. What is the face value of your investment in the zero-coupon bond?

13. Describe cash flow matching and a dedication strategy and how each may be used to immunize a portfolio.

14. You manage a portfolio that has a minimum acceptable terminal value of $21 million in 4 years. Today's interest rate is 8%. You want to use a contingent immunization strategy. Consider each case separately.
    a. What is the trigger point for the portfolio value today? If the portfolio is worth $16 million should you immunize?
    b. Suppose that one year has passed and the interest rate is 7.3%. What is the trigger point? If the portfolio is worth $16 million should you immunize?
    c. Suppose that another year has passed and the interest rate is 8.7%. What is the trigger point? If the portfolio's value is $17.8 million should you immunize?
    d. Another year has passed and the interest rate is 9.4%. What is the trigger point? If the portfolio's value is $19 million should you immunize?

15. Classify each of the following types of swaps.
    a. selling a bond that has a duration of 4.3 years and buying a bond that has a duration of 5.8 years in an effort to increase return by holding longer-maturity bonds
    b. selling a bond that you purchased for par value and that is currently selling below par value to purchase another bond and realize a capital loss
    c. selling Southwestern Bell Communications bonds that have a 10-year maturity, a 5.2% coupon rate, and a yield to maturity of 6.3% and buying a Verizon bond that has the same maturity and coupon rate, but is selling for a yield of 6.7%
    d. selling a Treasury bond and buying a AA corporate bond because you believe the yield on the Treasury is too high relative to the yield on the AA corporate bond
    e. selling a Treasury bond with a 20-year maturity and buying a Treasury bond with a 10-year maturity because you believe that interest rates are going to fall

16. What are the six general properties regarding the interest rate sensitivity of bond prices?

17. What are the five rules of duration?

Chapter 17
Macroeconomic and Industry Analysis

1. Define the following terms:
   a. Gross Domestic Product
   b. Unemployment Rate
   c. Inflation

2. What is "crowding out"?

   Refer to the following information in answering questions 3 through 8 below.

   Two firms, A and B, both produce brushes. The price of brushes is $1.20 each. Firm A has total fixed costs of $450,000 and variable costs of 48 cents per brush. Firm B has total fixed costs of $260,000 and variable costs of 72 cents per brush. The corporate tax rate is 30%. If the economy is strong, each firm will sell 1,500,000 brushes. If the economy enters a recession, each firm will sell 980,000 brushes.

3. If the economy enters a recession, the after-tax profit of Firm A will be _____.

4. If the economy enters a recession, the after-tax profit of Firm B will be _____.

5. If the economy is strong, the after-tax profit of Firm A will be _____.

6. If the economy is strong, the after-tax profit of Firm B will be _____.

7. Calculate firm A's degree of operating leverage.

8. Calculate firm B's degree of operating leverage.

9. Define the following terms:
   a. peak
   b. trough
   c. cyclical industry
   d. defensive industry

10. What are leading, lagging, and coincident economic indicators? To which group does each of the following belong?
    a. industrial production
    b. money supply (M2)
    c. new orders for nondefense capital goods
    d. change in the consumer price index for services
    e. initial claims for unemployment insurance
    f. average duration of unemployment
    g. manufacturing and trade sales
    h. new private housing units authorized by local building permits
    i. ratio of consumer installment credit outstanding to personal income

11. What three factors determine the sensitivity of a firm's earnings to the business cycle? How does each one influence earnings?

12. List and describe the four stages in the industry life cycle.

13. List and describe Porter's five determinants of competition.

14. What are the two broad classes of macroeconomic tools that the governments can use to affect the economy?

15. What is sector rotation and why is macro economic and industry analysis important in determining the asset allocation?

16. Discuss the ways in which the global economy might have an effect on a firm whose headquarters are in Oklahoma. Be specific – cite some of the relevant factors that should be considered.

17. A junior analyst was assigned the task of examining potential supply and demand and demand shocks and their affect on the macro-economy. Briefly explain what these shocks are and give a few examples of both positive and negative shocks.

Chapter 18
Equity Valuation Models

1. Define the following terms that can be used to measure the value of a company:
   a. book value
   b. liquidation value
   c. replacement cost
   d. Tobin's q

2. MN Tool Company has an expected ROE of 11%. The dividend growth rate will be _____ if the firm follows a policy of paying 25% of earnings in the form of dividends.

3. A preferred stock will pay a dividend of $4.16 in the upcoming year, and every year thereafter, i.e., dividends are not expected to grow. You require a return of 10% on this stock. Use the constant growth DDM to calculate the intrinsic value of this preferred stock.

4. You are considering acquiring a common stock that you would like to hold for one year. You expect to receive both $1.41 in dividends and $33 from the sale of the stock at the end of the year. The maximum price you will pay for the stock today is _____ if you want to earn an 11% return.

Use the following information to answer questions 5 through 7.

Monarch Marketing Company is expected to pay a dividend of $2.25 in the upcoming year. The risk-free rate of return is 4.25% and the expected return on the market portfolio is 12.5%. Analysts expect the price of Monarch Marketing Company shares to be $23 a year from now. The beta of Monarch Marketing Company's stock is 1.35.

5. The required rate of return on Monarch Marketing Company's stock is _____.

6. What is the intrinsic value of Monarch Marketing Company's stock today?

7. If Monarch Marketing Company's price is $21.00 today, what must be its expected growth rate?

8. Easy Ride Airlines is expected to pay a dividend of $3 in the coming year. Dividends are expected to grow at the rate of 10% per year. The risk-free rate of return is 5% and the expected return on the market portfolio is 12%. The stock of Easy Ride has a beta of 1.5. The return you should require on the stock is _____. If beta doubled to 3.0, would the required return double?

9. Moderate Growth Company paid a dividend last year of $2.00. The expected ROE for next year is 13%. An appropriate required return on the stock is 11%. If the firm has a plowback ratio of 65%, the dividend in the coming year should be _____.

10. a. According to the dividend discount model, what is the relationship between intrinsic value and each of the following:
   - the level of dividends per share
   - the market capitalization rate
   - the expected growth rate of dividends
   b. What does the constant growth model imply about the growth rate of the stock price relative to the growth rate of the dividends?

11. Suppose that the average P/E multiple in the health care industry is 22. Health Southwest is expected to have an EPS of $2.00 in the coming year. The intrinsic value of Health Southwest stock should be _____.

12. An analyst has determined that the intrinsic value of Dapper Dugouts stock is $20 per share using the capitalized earnings model. If the typical P/E ratio in this industry is 32, then it would be reasonable to assume the expected EPS of Dapper Dugouts in the coming year is_____.

13. Saks is expected to pay a dividend in year 1 of $1.65, a dividend in year 2 of $1.97, and a dividend in year 3 of $2.54. After year 3, dividends are expected to grow at the rate of 8% per year. An appropriate required return for the stock is 11%. The stock should be worth _____ today.

14. Declining Products Corporation produces goods that are very mature in their product life cycles. Declining Products Corporation is expected to pay a dividend in year 1 of $1.00, a dividend of $0.90 in year 2, and a dividend of $0.85 in year 3. After year 3, dividends are expected to decline at a rate of 2% per year. An appropriate required rate of return for the stock is 8%. The stock should be worth _____.

15. Why do some stocks have relatively high values when they have relatively low, or even negative, earnings?

16. What are some other ratios that can be used as alternatives to the P/E ratio for comparative valuation?

17. Discuss the free cash flow approach to firm valuation. How does it compare to the dividend discount model (DDM)?

18. Bushhog Corporation is expected have EBIT of $800k this year. Bushhog Corporation is in the 30% tax bracket, will report $52,000 in depreciation, will make $86,000 in capital expenditures, and have a $16,000 increase in net working capital this year. What is Bushhog's FCFF?

Chapter 19
Financial Statement Analysis

Refer to the financial statements of the Heavy Hog Company below in answering questions 1 through 11.

2007 Income Statement

Sales	$ 5,600,000
Cost of Goods Sold	3,600,000
Depreciation Expense	500,000
Gross Profit	$ 1,500,000
Selling and Admin. Expenses	515,000
Operating Income	$ 985,000
Interest Expense	60,000
Taxable Income	$ 925,000
Tax	225,000
Net Income	$ 700,000

Comparative Balance Sheets

	2007	2006
Cash	$ 83,000	$ 40,000
Accounts Receivable	557,000	450,000
Inventory	931,000	700,000
Total Current Assets	$ 1,571,000	$ 1,190,000
Gross Fixed Assets	2,319,000	1,500,000
Accumulated Depreciation	800,000	300,000
Net Fixed Assets	1,519,000	1,200,000
Total Assets	$ 3,090,000	$ 2,390,000
Accounts Payable	$ 312,000	$ 200,000
Notes Payable	525,000	500,000
Total Current Liabilities	$ 837,000	$ 700,000
Long-Term Debt	875,000	1,000,000
Total Liabilities	$ 1,712,000	$ 1,700,000
Common Stock (20,000 shares)	200,000	200,000
Retained Earnings	1,178,000	490,000
Total Equity	$ 1,378,000	$ 690,000
Total Liabilities & Equity	$ 3,090,000	$ 2,390,000

1. Calculate Heavy Hog's current ratio for 2007.

2. Calculate Heavy Hog's quick ratio for 2007.

3. Calculate Heavy Hog's leverage ratio for 2007.

4. Calculate Heavy Hog's times interest earned ratio for 2007.

5. Calculate Heavy Hog's average collection period ratio for 2007.

6. Calculate Heavy Hog's inventory turnover ratio for 2007.

7. Calculate Heavy Hog's fixed asset turnover ratio for 2007.

8. Calculate Heavy Hog's total asset turnover ratio for 2007.

9. Calculate Heavy Hog's return on sales ratio for 2007.

10. Calculate Heavy Hog's return on equity ratio for 2007.

11. Construct a Statement of Cash Flows for Heavy Hogs for the year 2007. Is the firm in a healthy financial position with regard to cash flows? Summarize the results by discussing how Heavy Hogs is getting and using its cash.

12. What is the difference between accounting earnings and economic earnings?

13. Calculate the economic value added (EVA) for each of the firms listed. What factors might cause a negative EVA?

	Capital (millions)	Return on Assets	Cost of Capital
Alpha Athletics	$7.43	11.00%	9.00%
Beta Body Builders	$19.25	-3.00%	16.00%
Lambda Levitators	$6.47	26.00%	18.00%
Theta Theoretics	$2.23	24.00%	14.00%

14. What is the difference between accounting depreciation and economic depreciation? Does the use of accounting depreciation present a bias for analysts?

15. What are some of the items that can affect a firm's quality of earnings? Briefly explain how the treatment of each item might change your assessment of earnings quality.

16. What is the DuPont system and why is it useful? What is the formula? Enter the formula that corresponds to the description of each ratio into the second column of the table. The third column gives a value for each ratio. Use the fourth column to describe the meaning of the ratio's value.

Tax Burden		0.60	
Margin		0.10	
Leverage		1.67	
Turnover		1.00	
Interest Burden		0.68	

17. What is common-size analysis and why is it useful? How are common-size financial statements prepared.

Chapter 20
Options Markets: Introduction

1. a. You have just purchased the options listed below. Based on the information given, indicate whether the option is in the money, out of the money, or at the money, whether you should exercise the option if it were expiring today, what the dollar profit would be, and what the percentage return would be.

Company	Option	Strike	Today's stock price	In/Out of the Money?	Premium	Exercise?	Profit	Return
ABC	call	10	10.26		1.10			
ABC	put	10	10.26		0.95			
XYZ	call	25	23.93		1.05			
XYZ	put	25	23.93		2.25			

   b. Now suppose that time has passed and the stocks' prices have changed as indicated in the table below. Recalculate your answers to part a.

Company	Option	Strike	Today's stock price	In/Out of the Money?	Premium	Exercise?	Profit	Return
ABC	call	10	11.23		1.10			
ABC	put	10	11.23		0.95			
XYZ	call	25	27.00		1.05			
XYZ	put	25	27.00		2.25			

2. Discuss how each of the following items differs for options that are traded over the counter vs. on standardized exchanges:
   - terms of the contract
   - costs
   - depth of trading
   - ease of trading and liquidity

3. a. How is the value of a call option related to its exercise price and to the price of the underlying stock?
   b. How is the value of a put option related to its exercise price and to the price of the underlying stock?

4. Discuss the following features of the Option Clearing Corporation (OCC):
   - ownership
   - relationship to options traders
   - interaction with member firms
   - margin requirements

5. You write one GE 60 put for a premium of $4. Ignoring transactions costs, what is the breakeven price of this position?

6. You purchase one Wal-Mart 60 call option for a premium of $3. Ignoring transaction costs, the breakeven price of the position is _____.

7. a. Suppose that you purchased a call option with a strike price of $30 and paid a premium of $6. Draw a graph of what your payoff and profit would be at expiration for stock prices in the range of $10 to $70.
   b. Now assume that instead of purchasing the call you wrote the option. Draw a graph of what your payoff and profit would be from this perspective.

Refer to the following information to answer questions 8 through 11.

Suppose you purchase one Sears May 20 call contract at $2 and write one Sears May 25 call contract at $1:

8. The maximum potential profit of your strategy is _____.

9. If, at expiration, the price of a share of Sears stock is $23, what would your profit be?

10. The maximum loss you could suffer from your strategy is _____.

11. What is the lowest stock price at which you can break even?

Refer to the following information to answer question 12 and 13.

You buy one JNJ Apr 55 call contract and one JNJ Apr 55 put contract. The call premium is $1 and the put premium is $4.

12. Your maximum loss from this position could be _____.

13. At expiration, you break even if the stock price is equal to _____.

14. IBM Stock currently sells for $80. A one-year call option with strike price of $86 sells for $7, and the risk free interest rate is 4%. What is the price of a one-year put with strike price of $86?

15. Consider a one-year maturity call option and a one-year put option on the same stock, both with a strike price $90. If the risk-free rate is 4%, the stock price is $92, and the put sells for $6, what should be the price of the call?

16. What is the difference between American and European options?

17. Explain the major characteristics of the following types of exotic options:
    a. Asian
    b. Barrier
    c. Lookback
    d. Digital
    e. Currency-translated

18. Explain the following option strategies:
    a. covered call
    b. protective put
    c. straddle
    d. strips
    e. straps
    f. spread
    g. collar

Chapter 21
Option Valuation

1. Use the two-state put option valuation model for this problem. $S_0 = \$50$; $X = \$55$; the two possibilities for S_T are \$65 and \$45. The range of P across the two states is _____; the hedge ratio is _____.

2. You plan to buy a stock that is currently selling for \$50. You forecast that in one year, the stock's price will be either \$70 or \$30, with equal probabilities. There is a one-year call option on the stock available with an exercise price of \$60. You are able to borrow at a rate of 9%. You would like to hedge your stock position using the call option.
   a. What will be the call's value if the stock price is \$70 in one year? What will be the call's value if the stock price is \$30 in one year?
   b. What is the hedge ratio?
   c. Assume that you can purchase fractional shares of stock. How many shares of stock would you buy? What position would you take in the option?
   d. What will be the value of your portfolio (combined stock and option position) in one year if the stock's price turns out to be \$70? What will be the value of your portfolio if the stock's price turns out to be \$30?
   e. What is the present value of the amount you found in part d?
   f. What is the value of the call option today?

3. Suppose that the call option from problem 2 is actually selling for \$6.20. How could you combine options with one share of stock to make arbitrage profits? Fill in the entries in the table below to illustrate the cash flows and payoffs to this strategy. Why does this constitute an arbitrage opportunity?

	Initial Cash Flow	Cash Flow in One Year	
		S = \$30	S = \$70
Options Market			
Stock Market			
Borrowing/Lending			
Total CF			

4. In the Black-Scholes option pricing model, what assumptions are made about the following items?
   a. the risk-free interest rate
   b. stock price volatility
   c. the expected rate of return on the stock
   d. dividend yield
   e. the stock's price

5. Use the Black-Scholes Option Pricing Model for this problem. Given: $S_0 = \$70$; $X = \$75$; T = 365 days; r = 0.06 annually; $\sigma = 0.45$. No dividends will be paid before option expires. The value of the call option is _____.

   Refer to the following information to answer questions 6 through 9.

   A European call option with six months to maturity has a strike price of $44. The underlying stock now sells for $52. The call premium is $10.

6. What is the intrinsic value of the call?

7. What is the time value of the call?

8. If the option has delta of .5, what is its elasticity?

9. If the risk-free rate is 6%, what should be the value of a put option on the same stock with the same strike price and expiration date?

10. Portfolio A consists of 200 shares of stock and 100 calls on that stock. Portfolio B consists of 250 shares of stock. The call delta is 0.6. Which portfolio has a higher dollar exposure to a change in stock price?

11. A portfolio consists of 500 shares of stock and 300 calls on that stock. If the hedge ratio for the call is 0.6, what would be the dollar change in the value of the portfolio in response to a one dollar decline in the stock price?

12. If the hedge ratio for a stock call is 0.70, the hedge ratio for a put with the same expiration date and exercise price as the call would be _____.

13. A put option is currently selling for $4 with an exercise price of $40. If the hedge ratio for the put is –0.40 and the stock is currently selling for $39, what is the elasticity of the put?

14. You have used the Black-Scholes model to calculate a value of $0.45 for a call option. When you checked the value of the option on line you found a value of $0.52 listed. What factor is most likely to account for the difference in the prices?

15. What is dynamic hedging? Why might it contribute to market volatility?

16. Define the following terms:
    a. gamma
    b. delta neutral
    c. volatility risk
    d. implied volatility
    e. delta or hedge ratio

17. Discuss the relationship between option prices and time to expiration, volatility of the underlying stocks, and the exercise price.

Chapter 22
Futures Markets

1. Define the following terms as they relate to futures contracts:
   a. futures price
   b. settlement price
   c. spot price
   d. reversing trade
   e. marking to market
   f. basis

2. Explain how a clearinghouse works to ensure the fulfillment of futures contract obligations.

3. Answer the questions below based on the listing shown for the July orange juice futures contract.

Orange Juice (NYBOT) - 15,000 lbs.; cents per lb.

	Open	High	Low	Settle	Change	Lifetime High	Lifetime Low	Open Interest
Nov	175.00	175.50	172.60	174.00	0.95	176.95	108.00	8,946

   a. Where is the contract traded?
   b. What is the current total value of a position in the contract based on the settle price?
   c. What was the previous day's settle price?
   d. What is the maximum price that was paid for the contract during its lifetime?
   e. How many of the December wheat contracts are outstanding?
   f. If you take a short position in the contract, what will your responsibilities be?

4. Suppose that the current price of a gold futures contract is 650.00 dollars per troy oz., with contract units specified as 100 troy oz. Calculate the profit for a long position in the futures contract for the following possible spot prices at the expiration date. Ignore transactions costs. Draw a graph that shows the profit for each of these spot prices.

Spot Price at Maturity	550.00	600.00	650.00	700.00	750.00
Profit to Long Position					

5. You purchased a Treasury bond futures contract on the Chicago Board of Trade (CBOT) at a futures price of 97-08. What would your profit (loss) be at maturity if the futures price increased by 1 point? Ignore transactions costs.

6. On January 1, the listed spot and futures prices of a Treasury bond were 94-6 and 96-15. You purchased $100,000 par value Treasury bonds and sold one Treasury bond futures contract. One month later, the listed spot price and futures prices were 96 and 96.22, respectively. If you were to liquidate your position, your profits would be? Ignore transactions costs.

7. You purchased one silver futures contract at $3.15 per ounce. What would be your profit or loss at maturity if the silver spot price at that time is $3.05 per ounce? Assume the contract size is 5,000 ounces and there are no transactions costs.

8. You sold one silver futures contract at $3.15 per ounce. What would be your profit or loss at maturity if the silver spot price at that time is $3.05 per ounce? Assume the contract size is 5,000 ounces and there are no transactions costs.

9. On July 1, you bought one S&P 500 index futures contract at a price of 990. On September 15th the futures price is 1018. What would be your profit or loss if you closed your position? Assume that there are no transactions costs.

10. Given a stock index with a value of 1,200, an anticipated dividend of $45 and a risk-free rate of 4%, what should be the value of one futures contract on the index?

Refer to the following information in answering questions 11 through 14.

You purchased the following futures contract today at the settlement price listed in the Wall Street Journal. Answer the questions below regarding the contract.

Corn (CBT) 5,000 bu.; cents per bu					Lifetime		
	Open	High	Low	Settle	Change	High	Low	Open Interest
Nov.	204.5	206.75	204	204	+3.5	268.5	182	3,095

11. What is the total value of the futures contract?

12. If there is a 10% margin requirement how much do you have to deposit?

78

13. Suppose the price of the futures contract changes as shown in the following table. Enter the relevant information into the table (show your calculations).

Day	Futures Price	Profit/Loss per bu.	Total Value of Contract	Mark-to-Market Settlement
0	204.0	n.a.		n.a.
1	204.6			
2	206.0			
3	203.9			

14. Explain why the account is marked-to-market daily.

15. You are managing a portfolio that has $500,000 in Treasury notes. The current price for a 6-month T-note futures contract is 104. You are concerned that T-note prices might be as low as 94 and as high as 114 in six months and want to protect your portfolio with a short hedge. How would you enact the hedge?

   Calculate the value of the T-note holdings and the profit or loss from the futures hedge in six months for T-note prices of 94, 104, and 114. Calculate the total value of your position for each price to show how the hedge is effective.

	T-Note Price in 6 months		
	94	104	114
Value of T-note Holdings			
Profits or Losses from Futures			
Total Value			

16. What is meant by the phrases "take a long position" and "take a short position"? What are the traders committing to?

17. What are contango, normal backwardation, the expectation hypothesis, and the convergence property?

Chapter 23
Futures, Swaps, and Risk Management

1. If you purchased one S&P 500 Index futures contract at a price of 950 and closed your position when the index futures were 922, your profit was _____.

2. If you took a short position in four S&P 500 futures contracts at a price of 925 and closed the position when the index futures were 884, your profit was _____.

3. Suppose that the risk-free rates in the United States and in Singapore are 4% and 8%, respectively. The spot exchange rate between the US dollar and the Singapore dollar is currently $0.633 US / $1 Singapore. What should the futures price of the Singapore dollar for a three month contract be to prevent arbitrage opportunities? Ignore transactions costs.

Refer to the following information in answering questions 4 through 6 below.

Risk-free rate in the United States	0.04/year
Risk-free rate in Australia	0.03/year
Spot exchange rate	US$0.52 /AUS$

4. What should be the proper futures price for a 1-year contract?

5. If the futures market price is $0.50 /A$, how can you execute an arbitrage strategy?

6. If the market futures price is $0.60 /A$, how can you execute an arbitrage strategy?

Refer to the following information in answering questions 7 through 10 below.

You are given the following information about a portfolio you are to manage. For the long-term you are bullish, but you think the market may fall over the next month.
A futures contract on the S&P 500 for the month is priced at 1025.

Portfolio Value	$1 million
Portfolio's Beta	1.22
Current S&P500 Value	1025
Anticipated S&P500 Value	960

7. If the anticipated market value materializes, what will be your expected loss on the portfolio?

8. What is the dollar value of your expected loss?

9. What would be your gain (loss) on the futures contract if your expectations are realized?

10. How many contracts should you buy or sell to hedge your position? Allow fractions of contracts in your answer.

11. Explain how to create a synthetic stock position using stock index futures. What are the advantages of doing this instead of buying the stocks?

12. You manage a portfolio with $1 million face value, 7% coupon, 20-year bonds and want to hold a short futures position to protect against excessive losses in the event of an increase in market rates. The T-bond futures contract calls for the delivery of an 8% coupon 20-year maturity bond. Assume annual payment of coupon interest on both bonds.
    a. What is the current value of your bond portfolio if the market interest rate is 9%?
    b. What is the current value of the $1 million face value, 8% delivery bond?
    c. If the market rate changes to 10.5%, what will be the value of your bond portfolio? What is the amount of your loss?
    d. What will be the value of the 8% delivery bond at a market rate of 10.5%? What is the amount of the change in value on this bond?
    e. Approximately how many futures contracts should you short to enact the hedge?

13. What is index arbitrage? How do transaction costs and program trading play a role in its implementation?

14. You are managing a portfolio of long-term bonds that have a face value of $50 million and a coupon rate of 6.4%. You think that interest rates will rise over the next month. What will happen to the value of the portfolio if this happens? Show how you can use an interest rate swap to reduce the risk.

15. The difference between the spot and futures (or forward) price of a currency occurs when there is an interest rate differential between the two countries. If interest rates differ, that difference must be offset by the forward (or futures) premium or discount. If this offset occurs, you are in a state of interest rate parity. When interest rate parity occurs, covered interest arbitrage is not possible. If the forward (futures) premium or discount does not offset the interest rate differential, it is possible to engage in covered interest arbitrage. This arbitrage will continue until exchange rates [spot and or forward (future)] realign such that the difference in interest rates is offset by price differences between spot and forward (futures) markets.

16. Direct quotes are expressed as the U.S. dollar price of one unit of foreign currency whereas indirect quotes are expressed as the number of foreign currency units that can be purchased for one U.S. dollar. Direct and indirect quotes are reciprocals.

Chapter 24
Portfolio Performance Evaluation

1. Suppose you buy 100 shares of Applied Materials Corporation at the beginning of year 1 for $42. Applied Materials Corporation pays no dividends. The stock price at the end of year 1 is $46, the price is $54 at the end of year 2, and the price is $62 at the end of year 3. The stock price declines to $59 at the end of year 4, and you sell your 100 shares. Your geometric average return for the four-year period is

    _____.

2. Suppose you purchase one share of the stock of Red Devil Corporation at the beginning of year 1 for $42. At the end of year 1, you receive a $2 dividend, and buy one more share for $46. At the end of year 2, you receive total dividends of $4 (i.e., $2 for each share), and sell the shares for $54.00 each. The time-weighted return on your investment is _____.

3. Suppose you purchase one share of the stock of Red Devil Corporation at the beginning of year 1 for $42. At the end of year 1, you receive a $2 dividend, and buy one more share for $46. At the end of year 2, you receive total dividends of $4 (i.e., $2 for each share), and sell the shares for $54.00 each. The dollar-weighted return on your investment is _____.

4. Interpret the data in the following chart, which represents the performance of municipal bond funds. The "♦" marks show the performance of the portfolio that you manage.

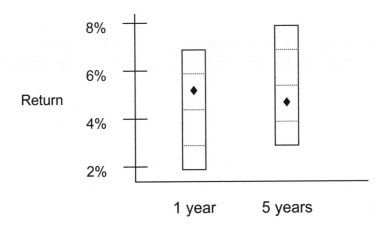

Use the following data to answer questions 5 through 10 regarding the performance of Guardian Stock Fund and the market portfolio. The risk-free return during the sample period was 5%.

	Guardian	Market Portfolio
Average Return	14%	10%
Standard Deviation of Returns	26%	21%
Beta	1.20	1.00
Residual Standard Deviation	4%	0%

5. Calculate Sharpe's measure of performance for Guardian Stock Fund.

6. Calculate Treynor's measure of performance for Guardian Stock Fund.

7. Calculate Jensen's measure of performance for Guardian Stock Fund.

8. Calculate the information ratio measure of performance for Guardian Stock Fund.

9. Calculate the M^2 measure of performance for Guardian Stock Fund.

10. Draw a graph that shows the CML and the CAL based in the data above. Show the positions of the market portfolio (M), the Guardian Stock Fund (P), and the hypothetical portfolio (P*, which you constructed to answer question 9) on the graph. Point out the distance that represents M^2 on the graph.

11. When is it appropriate to use the Sharpe measure or the M^2 measure? When would it be better to use the Treynor measure or the Jensen measure?

Use the following information to answer questions 12 through 14.

In a particular year, Growth Fund earned a return of 9% by making the following investments in asset classes.

	Weight	Return
Bonds	20%	5%
Stocks	80%	10%

The return on a bogey portfolio was 6.5%, calculated from the following information.

	Weight	Return
Bonds (Lehman Brothers Index)	50%	4%
Stocks (S&P 500 Index)	50%	9%

12. The total excess return on the Growth Fund's managed portfolio was _____.

13. The contribution of asset allocation across markets to the Growth Fund's total excess return was _____.

14. The contribution of selection within markets to the Growth Fund's total return was _____.

15. Describe the Morningstar Risk-Adjusted Rating (RAR) system. How does Morningstar determine how many stars a fund should earn?

16. What are the challenges in evaluating the performance of hedge funds?

17. What performance evaluation issues arise when a portfolio manager engages in market timing? How can these be overcome?

Chapter 25
International Diversification

1. How are emerging markets and developed markets defined? What percentage of total world capitalization did the top six developed countries make up in 2000? What percentage did they make up in 2005? What impact might this have on portfolio management decisions?

2. What is the major requirement stated by deSoto (2000) for economic advancement of a country? How does market capitalization relative to Gross Domestic Product (GDP) relate to the economic well-being of a country's population?

3. The yield on a 1-year bill in the UK is 6% and the present exchange rate is 1 pound = US $1.66. If you expect the exchange rate to be 1 pound = US $1.62 a year from now, the return a US investor can expect to earn by investing in UK bills is _____.

4. Suppose the 1-year risk-free rate of return in the U. S. is 4%. The current exchange rate is 1 pound = U. S. $1.66. The 1-year forward rate is 1 pound = $1.57. What is the minimum yield on a 1-year risk-free security in Britain that would induce a U. S. investor to invest in the British security?

5. The interest rate on a 1-year Canadian security is 5%. The current exchange rate is C$ = US $0.75. The 1-year forward rate is C$ = US $0.79. The return (denominated in U. S. $) that a U. S. investor can earn by investing in the Canadian security is _____.

6. Suppose the 1-year risk-free rate of return in the U. S. is 4% and the 1-year risk-free rate of return in Britain is 6%. The current exchange rate is 1 pound = U. S. $1.62. A 1-year future exchange rate of _____ for the pound would make a U. S. investor indifferent between investing in the U. S. security and investing the British security.

7. The present exchange rate is C$ = U. S. $0.75. The one year future rate is C$ = U. S. $0.76. The yield on a 1-year U. S. bill is 3.5%. A yield of _____ on a 1-year Canadian bill will make investor indifferent between investing in the U. S. bill and the Canadian bill.

Refer to the following information to answer questions 8 and 9 below.

Assume there is a fixed exchange rate between the Canadian and U. S. dollar. The expected return and standard deviation of return on the U. S. stock market is 12% and 19%, respectively. The expected return and standard deviation on the Canadian stock market is 14% and 22%, respectively. The covariance of returns between the U. S. and Canadian stock markets is 1.7.

8. If you invested 50% of your money in the Canadian stock market and 50% in the US stock market, the expected return on your portfolio would be _____.

9. If you invested 50% of your money in the Canadian stock market and 50% in the US stock market, the standard deviation of return of your portfolio would be _____.

10. You are a U. S. investor who purchased British securities for 12,000 pounds one year ago when the British pound cost $1.60. No dividends were paid on the British securities in the past year. Your total return based on U. S. dollars was _____ if the value of the securities is now 14,625 pounds and the pound is worth $1.63.

11. What are some of the factors considered when assigning a risk rating to a country?

12. Discuss performance evaluation of international portfolio managers in terms of potential sources of abnormal returns.

Refer to the following information to answer questions 13 through 16.

The manager of Exotic International Fund uses EAFE as a benchmark. Last year's performance for the fund and the benchmark were as follows:

	EAFE Weight	Return on Equity Index	Currency Appreciation $(E_1/E_0 - 1)$	Exotic's Weight	Exotic's Return
Europe	.35	13%	4%	.40	19%
Australia	.15	22%	- 6%	.10	18%
Far East	.50	16%	8%	.50	32%

13. Calculate Exotic's overall performance.

14. Calculate Exotic's currency selection return contribution.

15. Calculate Exotic's country selection return contribution.

16. Calculate Exotic's stock selection return contribution.

17. The table below presents an excerpt of the data in Table 25.9 of the text for 2001-2005. After examining the data, what conclusions can you draw? What are the policy implications regarding international diversification?

Country	Returns in U.S. Dollars			Returns in Local Currency		
	Average Return	Standard Deviation	Correlation with U.S.	Average Return	Standard Deviation	Correlation with U.S.
U.K.	3.05	14.83	0.83	0.26	14.64	0.83
U.S.	0.63	14.89	1.00	0.63	14.89	1.00
Australia	14.36	16.10	0.38	7.93	9.67	0.23
Japan	6.09	18.74	0.43	6.42	16.84	0.45
Korea	29.14	31.11	0.72	23.85	28.66	0.73
Finland	0.74	36.09	0.70	−3.56	36.69	0.68
Czech Rep.	35.19	21.73	0.44	26.22	19.88	0.42
China	25.55	27.00	0.19	−9.13	19.94	0.10
Argentina	5.15	38.09	0.38	28.23	43.38	0.23
Turkey	28.49	56.15	0.73	36.37	44.51	0.31

Chapter 26
Hedge Funds

1. Explain the five major differences between hedge funds and mutual funds.

2. Explain the difference between a directional strategy and a non-directional strategy and give an example of a non-directional strategy.

3. What is a market neutral position? Are market neutral positions riskless? Explain why a market neutral strategy is risky or risk free.

   Refer to the following information in answering questions 4 through 13.

   Assume that you manage a $1.25 million portfolio that has a beta of 1.12. You believe that the alpha of the portfolio is a positive 2% per month and that the market is about to fall sharply. The value of the S&P 500 is currently 1400, the risk-free rate is 0.25% (per month), and futures contracts on the S&P 500 are available ($250 multiplier) and priced at the current S&P 500 price.

4. How can the return on your portfolio during the next month be described? Hint: what is the formula?

5. What would be the value of your portfolio if the market rose 5% during the next 30 days and there were no returns to firm-specific factors? What would be your dollar gain?

6. What would be the value of your portfolio if the market fell 10% during the next 30 days and there were no returns to firm-specific factors? What would be your dollar gain?

7. How can you create a market neutral position?

8. What would be your gain on the futures position if the market rose 5% during the next 30 days?

9. What would be your gain on the futures position if the market fell 10% during the next 30 days?

10. What would be your total return to the combined portfolio and futures position if the market rose 5% during the next 30 days?

11. What would be your total return to the combined portfolio and futures position if the market fell 10% during the next 30 days?

12. What insight do you gain from the preceding analysis?

13. Is this portfolio riskless?

Chapter 27
The Theory of Active Portfolio Management

There are no problems for Chapter 27

Chapter 28
Investment Policy and the Framework of the CFA Institute

1. What are the four major steps in making an investment decision?

2. What should be the central focus of portfolio objectives?

3. What factors act as constraints on the investment process?

4. What are the steps in determining asset allocation?

5. As an individual, what is the most important factor in goal setting?

6. Compare the liquidity needs of mutual funds, pension funds, and endowment funds.

7. What is the "prudent investor rule"?

8. Describe each of the following types of life insurance policies and summarize the portfolio needs of life insurance companies.
   a. whole-life
   b. term insurance
   c. variable life
   d. universal life

9. What are the two basic types of pension plans? Explain the basic characteristics of each type of pension plan.

10. List and briefly explain seven risks that investors face.

11. Assume that at retirement you have accumulated $650,000 in a variable annuity contract. The assumed investment return is 7.5% and your life expectancy is 18 years. What is the hypothetical constant annual benefit payment?

12. Assume that at retirement you have accumulated $650,000 in a variable annuity contract. The assumed investment return is 7.5% and your life expectancy is 18 years. If the first year's actual investment return is 9%, what is the starting benefit payment?

Refer to the information below to answer questions 13 through 16.

Richard is 48 years old and has accumulated $278,000 in his self-directed defined contribution pension plan. Each year he contributes $2,500 to the plan and his employer contributes an equal amount. Richard thinks he will retire at age 62 and figures he will live to age 86. The plan allows for two types of investments. One offers a 3% risk-free real rate of return. The other offers an expected return of 11% and has a standard deviation of 28%. Richard now has 25% of his money in the risk-free investment and 75% in the risky investment. He plans to continue saving at the same rate and keep the same proportions invested in each of the investments. His salary will grow at the same rate as inflation.

13. How much does Richard currently have in the safe account and how much in the risky account?

14. Of the total amount of new funds that will be invested by him and by his employer on his behalf, how much will Richard put into the safe account each year and how much into the risky account?

15. How much can Richard be sure of having in the safe account at retirement? Assume that the additional contributions to the account start one year from now.

16. How much can Richard expect to have in his risky account at retirement? Assume that the additional contributions to the account start one year from now.

17. a. You manage a defined benefit plan for Squeaky Clean Enterprises. The plan will be obligated to pay $25 million in benefits in 23 years. If you can earn a 9% rate of return on investments, how much would you need to have on deposit today to meet the goal?
    b. Suppose that instead of having to pay $25 million in 23 years you will need to pay $1.5 million each year, starting 7 years from today, for a period of 18 years. How much should you have in fund assets today to be able to meet this goal if you can earn a 9% rate of return on investments?

98

Chapter 1 Answers
The Investment Environment

1. Real assets are used to produce goods and services. Real assets include land, labor, and buildings. These generate income in the economy and determine both the material wealth and the productive capacity of the economy. Real assets appear on only one side of the balance sheet.

2. Financial assets are claims on real assets and income from them. Financial assets include stocks and bonds. These contribute indirectly to the productive capacity of the economy. Financial assets appear on both sides of the balance sheet.

3. a. a share of Google common stock - equity
    b. a Treasury bond - fixed-income
    c. a call option on Texas Instruments stock - derivative
    d. an IBM bond - fixed-income
    e. a gold futures contract - derivative
    f. a share of stock in a closely held corporation - equity

4. According to Table 1.1 in the text,
    a. Real assets make up _32.9%_ of total assets.
    b. Financial assets make up _61.1%_ of total assets.
    c. The largest component of real assets is _real estate_ .
    d. The four largest components of financial assets are _pension reserves_ , _equity in noncorporate businesses_ , _deposits_ , and _corporate equity_ .
    e. The largest component of liabilities is _mortgages_ .
    f. The net worth percentage is _80.7%_ .

5. Consumption timing allows flexibility between earnings and spending. Therefore, when we are younger we can consume more than we earn by borrowing money to buy things like homes and automobiles. As we age, we can invest so that we are able to retire someday and live off of our prior earnings. Financial assets allow for the storage of wealth for future use.

6. Allocation of risk allows various types of assets, with varying degrees of risk, to be issued by businesses based on their needs and chosen by investors based on their preferences. This enables firms to raise the capital they need and gives investors a choice of assets with varying risk-return characteristics.

7. Unlike a sole proprietorship, where the owners are the managers, the owners of a corporation are its common stockholders. The stockholders elect the board of directors, which hires the management team. Thus, the day-to-day management of the firm is carried out by parties other than the owners. This allows for stability through time as ownership changes and allows investors to have partial ownership of firms without having to carry out management tasks. The objective that is acceptable to all owners is for management to maximize the value of the firm's share price.

8. The agency problem is due to possible conflicts of interest between the owners of a firm (the shareholders) and their agents (the firm's managers). Managers might make choices that are not in the shareholders' best interests, like spending money on lavish offices and travel. Some possible solutions are to make managers' salaries dependent on the firm's performance, for boards of directors to oust poor managers, and for security analysts to monitor the firm closely and report on unfavorable performance.

9. The three sectors of the economy are firms, households, and governments.
   a. Firms are typically net borrowers as they seek to expand and require external resources to take on valuable projects.
   b. Households are typically net savers as they seek to use consumption timing to plan for longer-term financial requirements such as educating their children and investing for retirement. As such, they are interested in the risk and the after-tax returns on investments.
   c. Governments are typically net borrowers, but their needs depend on the current relationship between tax receipts and expenditures.

10. Financial intermediaries connect borrowers and lenders. Some examples of financial intermediaries are banks, credit unions, and insurance companies. Financial intermediaries issue their own securities and invest in the liabilities of other firms. As such they can:
    a. pool resources to spread management costs over a larger base, which reduces costs to individual investors.
    b. diversify investments because they are able to invest in more securities.
    c. develop expertise through the increased volume of business that they do.
    d. achieve economies of scale by spreading research costs over the pool.

11. According to Table 1.3 in the text
    a. Real (tangible) assets make up __1.1%__ of total assets.
    b. Financial assets make up __91.7%__ of total assets.
    c. The largest component of real assets is __equipment and premises__ .
    d. The two largest components of financial assets are __loans and leases__ and __investment securities__ .
    e. The two largest components of liabilities are __deposits__ and __borrowed funds__ .
    f. The net worth percentage is __10.1%__ .

12. According to Table 1.4 in the text
    a. Real assets make up __52.8%__ of total assets.
    b. Financial assets make up __47.2%__ of total assets.
    c. The two largest components of real assets are __real estate__ and __equipment and software__ .
    d. The two largest components of financial assets are __other__ and __trade and consumer credit__ .
    e. The two largest components of liabilities are __other__ and __bonds and mortgages__ .
    f. The net worth percentage is __57.0%__ .

13. Securitization is the process of creating a new security by pooling other financial assets such as loans, and selling the new security that represents a share in the pooled assets. Examples are mortgage pass-throughs like GNMAs, student loan pass-throughs like SLMAs, car loan pass-throughs, and credit card pass-throughs.

14. A primary market transaction is one in which securities are initially issued. Thus, the issuing firm receives the money and delivers the securities. The secondary market is where existing securities are traded. Thus, the firm that originally issued the securities receives no proceeds from the transaction. The individual who is selling the securities receives the money and in turn delivers the securities to the individual who is buying them.

15. Five ways for investors to diversify their portfolios globally are listed and discussed below.
    a. Investors can purchase American Depository Receipts (ADRs), which are certificates that are denominated in dollars and represent claims on bundles of underlying stock.
    b. Investors can directly purchase foreign securities offered for sale in dollars.
    c. Investors can purchase international mutual funds that invest in international securities.
    d. Investors can purchase derivatives on foreign securities
    e. Investors can purchase country ETFs such as World Equity Benchmark Shares (WEBS) or iShares which use the same structure as ADRs but allow investors to trade portfolios of foreign stocks of a selected country.

16. Asset allocation refers to the choice among broad asset classes such as stocks, bonds, real estate, and cash. Security selection refers to the choice of which security to hold within each asset class.

17. The two portfolio construction methods are "top-down" and "bottom-up." The top-down method starts with determining the asset allocation for each asset class and then deciding which securities to purchase within each asset class. The bottom-up method ignores the asset class a security is in and the most attractively valued securities are purchased for the portfolio regardless of the resulting asset mix.

Chapter 2 Answers
Asset Classes and Financial Instruments

1. a. Repurchase Agreement – short-term sale of government securities with an agreement to repurchase them at a higher price
   b. Federal Funds – funds in the accounts of commercial banks at the Federal Reserve Bank.
   c. Commercial Paper – short-term unsecured debt issued by large corporations
   d. Eurodollar – dollar-denominated deposits at foreign banks or foreign branches of American banks.
   e. T-bill - short-term debt of the U.S. government
   f. Bankers' Acceptance – an order to a bank by a customer to pay a sum of money at a future date.

2. a. You would pay the ask price of the dealer, 101 and 12/32 percent of par value, or 101.375% of $1,000, or $1,013.75.
   b. You would receive the bid price of the dealer, 101 and 7/32 percent of par value, or 101.21875% of $1,000, or $1,012.1875.

3. Treasury bills are short-term debt instruments of the U.S. government. Maturities include 28, 91, and 182 days are issued weekly through an auction process. The minimum investment is $1,000. Interest earned on T-bills is taxable at the federal level, but is exempt from state and local taxes. Interest on T-bills is earned on a discount basis – the investor pays less than the face value for the T-bill and gets the face value at maturity.

   Treasury notes have maturities up to 10 years and Treasury bonds have maturities over 10 years. The coupon rate determines the amount of the interest that is paid semi-annually. T-bonds may be callable at face value.

4. Commercial paper is short-term unsecured debt issued by large well-known corporations (typically nonfinancial) that has an original maturity of less than 270 days. Very often, commercial paper is backed by a bank line of credit. Asset-backed commercial paper is typically issued by financial firms, such as banks, and is used to raise funds to invest in other assets and these assets are used to back the asset-backed commercial paper.

5. State and local governments issue municipal bonds. Since the interest received is tax-free at both the federal and the state levels, state and local governments can pay lower interest rates to investors.

A general obligation bond is backed by the "full faith and credit" of the issuer. A revenue bond is issued to fund a specific project and interest payments are tied to the revenues from that project or the municipal agency responsible for the project. An industrial development bond is issued to finance a commercial enterprise, such as a factory that will be operated as a private firm.

6. Corporate bonds are taxable, therefore the after-tax return would be $r_c = 0.0967(1 - 0.25) = 0.0725$, or 7.25%.

   Since municipal bonds are free of federal tax the after-tax return is equal to the before-tax rate of return or $r_m = 0.0692 (1 - 0) = 6.92\%$.

7. The equivalent taxable yield is the yield divided by the quantity one minus the tax rate or $r_m / (1-t)$. Therefore, the equivalent taxable yield is $(0.087 / 0.75) = 11.6\%$.

8. For you to be indifferent, the after tax returns would need to be equal. Since only the corporate bond is taxed, $r_c (1-t) = r_m$ must hold. Therefore, $0.0632 = .0815(1-t)$, $(1-t) = 0.77546$, and $t = .2245$ or 22.45%.

9. To compute an equally-weighted return, add the returns and divide by the number of returns. Therefore, the equally-weighted return is $[17+(-13)+6]/3 = 3.33\%$.

10. The total before-tax income is the $4.50 dividend. Since the firm can exclude 70% of the dividends received on preferred stock from tax, the firm must pay tax on 30% of the dividend, or $(\$4.50 \times .3) = \$1.35$. The firm is in the 30% tax bracket, so the tax liability is $\$1.35 \times .3 = \$0.405$. Therefore, the firm nets (after tax) $\$4.50 - 0.405 = \$4.095$. Since the firm experienced no capital gain (or loss), the after tax return is $\$4.095 / \$65 = .0630$ or 6.30%.

11. a. The approximate combined income tax rate is 33% + 4% = 37%.
    b. The exact combined income tax rate can be calculated using the formula
       Exact combined rate $= 1 - (1 - t_{federal}) \times (1 - t_{state})$
       $$= 1 - (1 - .33) \times (1 - .04)$$
       $$= 35.68\%$$

       The exact combined rate is less than the approximate combined rate because it takes into account the fact that the state taxes paid are deducted before the federal taxes are calculated.
    c. The calculation of taxes for a person with $100 of taxable income is shown below.

Income Earned	$100.00
State Income Tax Owed (.04 × $100.00)	$ 4.00
Income Taxable by Federal Govt. ($100 − 4.00)	$ 96.00
Federal Income Tax Owed (.25 × $96.00)	$ 31.68
Net Income ($96.00 − 31.68)	$ 64.32
Total Tax Paid ($4.00 + 31.68)	$ 35.68
Combined Tax Rate ($35.68 / $100.00)	**35.68%**

The data for questions 11 through 13 are reproduced below.

Stock	Current Price	# of shares outstanding
Stock A	$35	2,000
Stock B	$82	4,500
Stock C	$21	1,600

12. A price-weighted index is constructed by adding the prices of the securities and dividing by the number of securities in the index ($35 + $82 + $21)/3 = $46.

13. A value-weighted index is computed by first computing the market value of each stock (price time the number of shares outstanding). Once each market value is computed, add the market values together and divide by the divisor. In this case it is [($35 × 2,000) + ($82 × 4,500) + ($21 × 1,600)] /1,000 = 472.60.

14. a. To compute the return of the price-weighted index you need to find the new prices of the stocks and then compute the average as follows:

   Stock A = [$35 × (1.18)] = $41.30
   Stock B = [$82 × (0.94] = $77.08
   Stock C = [$21 × (1.30)] = $27.30
   Average = (41.30 + 77.08 + 27.3) / 3 = $48.56.
   The change in the index value (return) is (48.56 − 46) / 46 = 5.565%.

   b. To compute the return of the value-weighted index you need to use the new prices to find the new value of the index. The return will be the change in the value of the index. In this case the new value is [($41.30 × 2,000) + ($77.08 × 4,500) + ($27.30 × 1,600)] /1,000 = 473.14. The old value was [($35 × 2,000) + ($82 × 4,500) + ($21 × 1,600)] /1,000 = 472.60. Therefore, the return is (473.14 − 472.60) / 472.60 = 0.114%.

   c. The return of an equally-weighted index is the sum of the return of each security in the index divided by the number of securities or [18% + (−6%) + 30%] / 3 = 14.00%.

15. The data are reproduced below.

	P_0	Q_0	P_1	Q_1
Stock A	$22	200	$22	200
Stock B	$15	400	$15	400
Stock C	$82	100	$41	200

a. The value of the price-weighted index of the three stocks at time 0 equals (22 + 15 + 82) / 3 = 39.67.

b. From time 0 to time 1 nothing fundamental changed for the stocks. Stocks A and B have the same prices and number of shares outstanding. Stock C has split 2 for 1 - its price is half of what it was before and there are twice as many shares outstanding. Therefore, the price-weighted index should be the same at time 1 as it was at time 0. The index should equal 39.67.

c. So we can solve for the new divisor using the equation
    (22 + 15 + 41) / d = 39.67. The new divisor, d, equals 1.97.

d. The return on the price-weighted index would be (39.67–39.67)/39.67 = 0%. There was no change in the value of the index.

16. a. A put option is a security that gives the holder the right, but not the obligation, to sell an asset at the exercise (strike) price on or before the expiration date.

b. A call option is a security that gives the holder the right, but not the obligation, to buy an asset at the exercise (strike) price on or before the expiration date.

c. A long position in a futures contract obligates the holder to deliver the underlying asset for a specified price on the expiration date.

d. A short position in a futures contract obligates the holder to purchase the underlying asset for a specified price on the expiration date.

17. A futures contract is for 5,000 bushels and the price quote is cents per bushel. Therefore, if you purchased a futures contract on corn at a futures price of 350.25 your financial outlay would be (5,000 × 3.5025 = $17,512.50). If the price was 362.25 at the time of expiration, the contract would be worth (5,000 × 3.6225 = $18,112.50). Thus, your profit is $18,112.50 – $17,512.50 = $600. If you would have been short the futures contract, your loss would be $600. The calculation is the same but the difference lies in the fact that if you were short the corn contract, you are required to deliver corn for the futures price. Since the price of corn rose, you received less for the corn than the price you must pay to purchase the corn for delivery. In this case you would receive the $17,512.50 and must pay the $18,112.50.

Chapter 3 Answers
How Securities Are Traded

1. The explicit cost is 5.8% × 1,000,000 shares × $34 per share = $1,972,000. Because the price jumped by $12 per share immediately after issue, the amount of the issue's value "left on the table," or its implicit cost, is $12 per share × 1,000,000 shares = $12,000,000. Of the $13,972,000 total cost, the implicit cost is much higher than the explicit cost.

2. a. New securities are offered to the public through the _primary_ market.
    b. In a(n) _auction_ market, buyers and sellers meet in one place to buy or sell assets.
    c. In a(n) _dealer_ market, the participants purchase assets for their own inventory, then sell them for a profit.
    d. Buyers and sellers must find each other on their own in a(n) _direct search_ market.
    e. When a security trades after its original issue date, the trade takes place in a(n) _secondary_ market.
    f. A(n) _brokered_ market is one in which an agent provides search services to match buyers and sellers.

3. a. Day
    b. Limit-buy
    c. Market
    d. Stop-buy

4. a. A stop sell (stop loss) order can be used to avoid bigger losses. A stop order is a defensive strategy.
    b. A limit sell order is an offensive strategy that may be used to take advantage of rising stock prices.

5. If you bought 400 shares @ $85/share, the cost was 400 × $85 = $34,000. Of this, you invested $34,000(.6) = $20,400 and borrowed $34,000 (1–0.60) = $13,600.

6. If you sold short 350 shares @ $42/share the proceeds were 350 × $42 = $14,700. With a margin of 60% you must have invested $14,700 × .6 = $8,820.

7. If you purchased 1000 shares @ $18 the cost was $18 × 1,000 = $18,000. Of this you invested 50% and borrowed 50%. Therefore, the loan amount was $18,000 × .5 = $9,000. Margin = Equity/Market Value = [1,000P – $9,000] / 1,000P. Therefore, 0.30 = (1,000P – $9,000)/1,000P; 300P = 1,000P – $9,000; –700P = –$9,000; P = $12.86

8. If you purchase 600 shares @ $27/share the cost is $27 × 600 = $16,200. Therefore, you invest 50% and borrow the other 50% of the amount. The loan amount is 16,200 × .5 = $8,100. Margin = [600 ($22) – $8,100] / 600 ($22); Margin = 0.386 or 38.6%.

9. The initial investment is 200($35)(0.50) = $3,500. The change in value of the stock is ($45.50 – $35)(200) = $2,100. Therefore, the return = $2,100 / $3,500 = 60%.

10. The profit on the stock is = ($30 – $37) (100) = – $700. The initial investment out of your own pocket equals the value of the stock times the initial margin percentage, ($100) (30) (.6) = $1,800. Therefore, the return is – $700 / $1,800 = –38.89%.

11. The amount in your account equals the cash you got from the short sale, 200($50) = $10,000, plus the cash required for margin, 200($50) × .5 = $5,000. Therefore total assets = $15,000. The amount of cash in your account doesn't change as the market price of the stock changes because you got cash when you short sold the stock. Total assets remain at $15,000 and your liability is the market value of the 200 shares of stock, or 200P. Therefore your net equity is total assets minus liabilities, or $15,000 – 200P. Margin = net equity / market value or 0.35 = ($15,000 – 200P) / 200P. Rearranging, 70P = 15,000 – 200P; 270P = 15,000; P = $55.56.

12. The amount in your account equals the cash you got from the short sale, 100($25) = $2,500, plus the cash required for margin, 100($25) × .5 = $1,250. Therefore total assets = $3,750. Your liability is the market value of 100 shares of stock. Therefore your net equity is $3,750 – 100P. Margin = net equity / market value or [$3,750 – 100 ($30)] / 100 ($30) = 25%.

13. The margin is 50% or = .5 = ($42Q–$2,700) / $42Q. Therefore, $21Q = $42Q – $2,700. Rearranging, –$21Q = –$2,700; Q = 128.54. Since you can only buy whole shares, you can buy 128 shares. Alternatively, you can buy [$2,700 (2)] / $42 = 128.57 shares.

14. The actual margin (AM) is equal to equity/market value. Equity equals the market value of the stock minus the amount you borrowed. Equity = [150 ($20) – (.45) (150) ($25)] = $1,312.50. [Remember, the initial margin percentage tells you how much of your own money must be invested, so the amount borrowed is based on 1 minus the initial margin percentage.] The market value of the stock after the price decline is [150 ($20)] = $3,000. Therefore, AM = $1,312.50 / $3,000 = .4375 or 43.75%.

15. a. Any compensation in addition to that received from the employer must be disclosed to the employer.
    b. Transactions for clients and employers must have priority over transactions of the member.
    c. Members shall not trade in the security if they have inside information.

16. Circuit breakers are the name for devices that interrupt trading on days when prices are too volatile. The purpose of circuit breakers is to temporarily interrupt trading so that market participants can fully digest relevant information to perhaps mitigate emotion-driven market swings. Trading halts are implemented if the DJIA falls by 10%. If the drop occurs before 2:00 p.m. EST, trading will be halted for 1 hour. If the drop occurs between 2:00 and 2:30, the halt will be for ½ hour. After 2:30, a 10% drop will not trigger a trading halt. There are also a variety of trading halts for a 20% drop. If the DJIA drops 30% at any time, the market will close for the remainder of the day.

17. The three broad practices that led to the financial scandals of 2000-2002 were centered on the allocation of shares in initial public offerings, tainted securities research, and recommendations disseminated to the public, and misleading financial statements. Regulatory response is still evolving but several initiatives have been implemented. Congress passed the Sarbanes-Oxley Act in 2002 to address the issue of misleading financial statements. The SEC's Regulation FD introduced in 2000 prohibits firms from releasing material information to one group (such as analysts) before being released to the public. Major investment banks agreed (in 2002) to separate their stock research and investment banking units to prevent conflicts of interest.

Chapter 4 Answers
Mutual Funds and Other Investment Companies

1. a. An investment company is a financial intermediary that accepts funds from individuals and pools the funds to invest in various types of securities.
    b. Investment companies perform record keeping and administration, diversification and divisibility, professional management, and lower transaction costs for investors.

2. NAV equals assets minus liabilities divided by the number of shares. Therefore, NAV = (750,000,000 – 8,000,000) / 40,750,000 = $18.21.

3. NAV = (Assets – Liabilities) / # of shares. Rearranging the equation, the number of shares equals the assets minus the liabilities divided by the NAV: ($316,000,000 – 42,000,000) / $28.64 per share = 9,567,039.11 shares.

4.

	Unit Investment Trust	Open-end Mutual Fund	Closed-end Mutual Fund
Management	unmanaged	managed	managed
Type of Assets	uniform, fixed	varied, changing	varied, changing
Fees	can be lower because of minimal management	loads, 12b-1, operating expenses	not explicit
Number of Shares	fixed	varies	fixed
Purchase	buy from trustee at a premium to NAV	buy from fund at NAV plus load, if any	buy in secondary market; price may differ from NAV
Redemption	sell to trustee for NAV	redeem to fund for NAV	sell in secondary market; price may differ from NAV

5. a. An index fund attempts to match the performance of a broad market index.
    b. A money market fund has a net asset value that is fixed at $1 per share and may offer a check-writing option.
    c. A balanced fund holds both equities and fixed-income securities in fairly stable proportions.
    d. An equity fund holds primarily stock, but may also hold fixed-income or other types of securities.
    e. An asset allocation fund holds both equities and fixed-income securities and varies the proportions to take advantage of forecasted market conditions.
    f. A specialized sector fund holds securities of firms in a particular industry or sector.
    g. A bond fund primarily holds fixed-income securities.
    h. A life cycle fund is a balanced fund in which the mix of securities depends on the age of the investor.

6. A front-end load is a fee that is paid when shares of the mutual fund are purchased. It is considered to be a commission or a sales charge. It reduces the amount of your effective investment and you will require a positive rate of return to break even. For example, if you send a check to the mutual fund and the front-end load is 5%, only 95% of the amount you sent will be invested initially.

    A back-end load is a fee you pay when you redeem your shares. It is also called a redemption fee, an exit fee, or a contingent deferred sales charge. It reduces the amount you receive when you cash in the shares. Over time, most mutual funds reduce the percentage of the exit fee you will have to pay. The longer you leave your funds invested in the fund, the lower the back-end fee.

7. The return is calculated by finding the change in value of the investment divided by the price. The change in value is the capital gain (whether realized or not) plus the sum of all distributions. Therefore, return = ($14.87 – 14.25 + .59 + 1.36) / $14.25 = 18.04%.

8. The return equals the change in NAV, $(NAV_1 - NAV_0)$, plus all distributions divided by the investment. Therefore, $0.142 = (NAV_1 - \$16.25 + 1.02 + 0.63) / \$16.25$; $NAV_1 = \$16.91$.

9. Turnover is the value of securities sold divided by the average assets of the fund. Therefore, 625,000,000 / 1,800,000,000 = 34.72% turnover.

10. Since the fund has a front load, only (1 − .0575) times NAV is actually invested and growing. Therefore the initial investment equals $18 × .9425 = $16.965. The money invested will grow at 12% minus the 0.75% fees (or 11.25%). The ending balance in your account will equal $16.97 × (1.1125) = $18.8736. Your initial out of pocket investment was $18.00, so your return is ($18.8736–18.00) / $18.00 = 4.85%.

11. NAV = Offer Price × (1-Load), so the offer price equals NAV divided by one minus load. Therefore, the offer price is $16.12 / (1 −.0562) = $17.08.

12. The offer price times one minus the load fee equals NAV. Therefore, NAV equals $14.77 × (0.94) = $13.88.

13. The value of assets is [($35 × 2,000) + ($82 × 4,500) + ($21 × 1,600)] = $472,600. Since NAV is asset minus liabilities divided by the number of shares outstanding, NAV = ($472,600 −$47,000) / 50,000 = $8.51.

14. Since both strategies have a claim on the same portfolio of securities, you need to compute your expected terminal wealth under each strategy.

    The terminal wealth (future value) of the no-load fund would be the initial investment, ($10,000), times one plus the net rate of return, (return minus 12-b1 fee), or 1.095 raised to the power N (N = number of years = 16). Therefore, the terminal value for this class equals $10,000 $(1.095)^{16}$ = $42,719.48.

    The terminal wealth of the front-load fund would be the initial investment in the portfolio, ($10,000) (1-load), times one plus the rate of return or 1.1025 raised to the power N (16). Therefore, the terminal value for this class is $9,500 $(1.1025)^{16}$ = $45,266.94.

    In this case, you would be better off with the load fund.

15. The full $5,000 would initially be invested in the Class A shares since there is no front-end load. The initial investment in Class B shares would be $5,000 × (1 − .055) = 4,725. The net return on the Class A shares equals the gross return of 6.8% minus the 2% expense ratio, or 4.8%. The net return on the Class B shares equals the gross return of 7.2% minus the 1.2% expense ratio, or 6%. The future values are calculated using the formula $FV_n = PV_0 \times (1+r)^n$.

Class A: $FV_4 = \$5,000 \times (1.048)^4 = \$6.031.36$

$FV_8 = \$5,000 \times (1.048)^8 = \$7,275.46$

Class B: $FV_4 = \$4,725 \times (1.06)^4 = \$5,965.20$

$FV_8 = \$4,725 \times (1.06)^8 = \$7,530.93$

	Class A	Class B
Initial Investment	$5,000.00	$4,725.00
Value after 4 years	$6.031.36	$5,965.20
Value after 8 years	$7,275.46	$7,530.93

If you plan to hold the shares for four years, you would prefer the Class A shares because they are worth more. There is no front load, so the full $5,000 starts working for you right away and this offsets the lower expected return. But if you plan to hold the shares for eight years you would prefer the Class B shares because they are worth $255.48 more by then. The front-end load you initially had to pay to invest in the Class B shares would be more than offset by the higher net return by this time.

16. Turnover measures the percentage of the portfolio that was replaced during the year. Turnover is important to investors because the sale of securities generates realized capital gains, and those gains will be subjected to income tax unless the security is held in a tax-deferred account (such as an IRA, 401k, 403b, or 457 plans). Moreover, those gains are not controllable by the investor. Thus, high turnover funds are not tax efficient. Funds with low turnover are called tax efficient because they generate few realized capital gains.

17. Superfund's turnover is the dollar value of assets sold (and replaced) divided by average assets. In this case $22M / $88M = .25 or 25%.

Chapter 5 Answers
Learning about Return and Risk from the Historical Record

1. The Fisher relation states that (1 + nominal rate) = (1 + real rate) (1 + Inflation). Therefore, the exact real rate of interest is r = (1 + nominal) / (1+ inflation) – 1 or 1.09 / 1.012 – 1 = 7.71%.

2. The approximate relationship states that nominal = real + inflation. Therefore, rearranging provides the approximate real interest rate which is 3% – 1.5% = 1.5%.

3. The approximate relationship states that (nominal) = (real) + inflation. Therefore, rearranging provides the approximate nominal interest rate which is 3% + 2% = 5%.

4. The approximate after tax real rate of return can be found by finding the after tax return and subtracting the inflation rate. The after tax nominal return is $3.5 \times (1–.33)$ = 2.345%. Once inflation is subtracted, the approximate after tax real return is 2.345 – 2.5 = –0.155%.

5. a. The relationship is $1 + EAR = \exp(r_{cc})$. Then $1 + EAR = e^{.07} = 107.25\%$, and EAR = 7.25%.
   b. To find r_{cc}, we can use the equation $\ln(1 + EAR) = r_{cc}$. For an EAR of 8.75%, remember to express the 8.75% in a decimal format and find $\ln(1.0875)$ = .0839. The continuously compounded rate is r_{cc} = 8.39%.

6. The HPR equals the change in wealth (dividend plus capital gain) divided by the purchase price or ($1.50 + $28 – $27) / $27 = 9.26%.

7. The expected HPR is the sum of the products of the probability of each state occurring times the expected return if that state occurs or 0.6 (19%) + .3 (13%) + .1 (–6%) = 14.7%.

8. The expected variance (σ^2) is the sum of the product of the probability of each state occurring times (the expected return if that state occurs minus the expected average return) squared or [.6 (19% – 14.7%)^2 + .3 (13% – 14.7%)^2 + .1 (–6% – 14.7%)^2] = 54.81%^{2}. [Note that the unit of measure for the variance is a percentage squared.]

Setting up the calculations in table format as show below may be helpful.

State	Probability	HPR (%)	HPR – E(HPR)	[HPR – E(HPR)]^2	Prob * [HPR – E(HPR)]^2
Boom	0.6	19.00	4.30	18.49	11.094
Normal growth	0.3	13.00	–1.70	2.89	0.867
Recession	0.1	–6.00	–20.70	428.49	42.849
				Variance =	54.81
HPR = 14.70% (from above)				Std. Deviation =	7.403

9. The expected standard deviation is (σ) is square root of the sum of the products of the probability of each state occurring times (the expected return if that state occurs minus the expected average return) squared or [.6 (19% – 14.7%)^2 + .3 (13% – 14.7%)^2 + .1 (–6% – 14.7%)^2]$^{1/2}$ = 7.40%. Or, once you have calculated the variance, the standard deviation is the square root of the variance. Standard deviation = (54.81%^{2})$^{1/2}$ = 7.40%.

10. The risk premium is equal to the expected return minus the risk-free rate or 14.7% – 3% = 11.70%.

11. To compute the expected return, first compute the expected selling price. The expected price $E(P_1)$ is equal to 0.25 ($55) + .40 ($62) + .35 ($71) = $63.40. Therefore, the E(HPR) = [($E(P_1)$ – P_0) + D]/ P_0 = ($63.40 – $50 + $3) / $50 = 32.80%.

12. The risk premium is equal to the expected return minus the risk-free rate. Therefore, the risk premium is 32.80% – 29.00% = 3.80%.

116

13.

Innovative Ideas Mutual Fund
Monthly Returns

January	3.49%
February	2.24%
March	− 2.17%
April	2.53%
May	4.48%
June	−0.04%

a. The arithmetic average return equals the sum of the months' returns divided by the number of months. The arithmetic return equals (3.49% + 2.24% − 2.17% + 2.53% + 4.48% − 0.04%) / 6 = 1.755%.

b. The geometric average return on the fund equals
$[(1+.0349) \times (1+.0224) \times (1-.0217) \times (1+.0253) \times (1+.0448) \times (1-.0004)]^{(1/6)} - 1$
$= [1.0349 \times 1.0224 \times 0.9783 \times 1.0253 \times 1.0448 \times 0.9996]^{0.166667} - 1$
= 1.730%

c. The arithmetic return of 1.755% is an unbiased estimate for the expected monthly return on the fund.

d. If you had invested $1,000 in the fund at the beginning of January, you would have $1,000 \times (1 + .01730)^6 = $1,108.41$ in your account at the end of June. The geometric average shows you the growth rate of your investment.

14. The Sharpe measure equals the risk premium divided by the standard deviation of excess returns. The risk premium equals the arithmetic average minus the risk-free rate, or 10.95% − 5.2% = 5.75%. The Sharpe measure is 5.75% / 8.49% = 0.677.

15. a. The interval that would contain 68.26% of the expected outcomes equals the expected return plus or minus one standard deviation.

   2.4% − 30.6% = −18.2%

   12.4% + 30.6% = 43.0%

   b. The interval that would contain 95.44% of the expected outcomes equals the expected return plus or minus two standard deviations.

   $12.4\% - 2 \times 30.6\% = -48.8\%$

   $12.4\% + 2 \times 30.6\% = 73.6\%$

   c. The interval that would contain 99.74% of the expected outcomes equals the expected return plus or minus three standard deviations.

   $12.4\% - 3 \times 30.6\% = -79.4\%$

   $12.4\% + 3 \times 30.6\% = 104.2\%$

16. a. The HPR equals $(2{,}585{,}0000 - 2{,}500{,}000)\,/\,2{,}500{,}000 = 3.40\%$

   b. There are $365/270 = 1.35185$ (rounded) 270-day periods in one year.

   c. The annual percentage rate APR is the 270-day rate times the number of 270-day periods in one year. $APR = 3.40\% \times 1.35185 = 4.60\%$.

   d. The EAR may be calculated either as

$$1 + EAR = (1 + \text{rate per period})^n = (1 + .034)^{1.35185} = 1.0462,\ EAR = 4.62\%$$

   or as

$$1 + EAR = \left(1 + \frac{APR}{n}\right)^n = \left(1 + \frac{.046}{1.35185}\right)^{1.35185} = 1.0462,\ EAR = 4.62\%$$

   e. The EAR is higher than the APR because it allows for compounding. It assumes that the investment will be repeated for the remainder of the year.

17. Testing for normality is important because if returns are not normally distributed (or approximately so), the standard deviation computed from those returns would not be a valid measure of risk. Two tests that can be used to examine normality are skewness and kurtosis.

   When the distribution is positively skewed, (skew statistic greater then zero), standard deviation overestimates risk. Conversely, the standard deviation of a negatively skewed distribution would underestimate risk.

   Kurtosis is a measure of fat tails. A kurtosis greater than zero indicates that the tails of the distribution are fatter than those of a normal distribution which would suggest a higher probability of higher or lower returns than expected from a normal distribution.

Chapter 6 Answers
Risk Aversion and Capital Allocation to Risky Assets

1. To be indifferent, the utility must be the same for both investments. Since the Treasury is riskless, its standard deviation is zero and its utility is its expected return, $U = .04$. Therefore, the utility of the risky investment must be .04. To solve the utility function for A, start with $.04 = .14 - .5 A (.25^2)$. Then $.04 - .14 = -(.5)A(.0625)$, and $-.10 = -.03125A$. Solving for A, we get $A = 3.2$. Check by plugging in an A value of 3.2 and see that utility equals 4: $U = .14 - (.5) (3.2) (.25^2) = .04 = U(r_f)$.

2. The utilities are presented below. Investment C would provide the highest utility to the investor described.

$$U(A) = .12 - (.5) (3) (.29^2) = -0.00615$$
$$U(B) = .15 - (.5) (3) (.35^2) = -0.03375$$
$$U(C) = .24 - (.5) (3) (.38^2) = \mathbf{0.02340}$$
$$U(D) = .29 - (.5) (3) (.44^2) = -0.00040$$

Note that the sign of the resulting calculations is not meaningful. Only the ranking is important, with the highest utility being the most favorable.

3. If you are risk neutral you would select investment D since your only concern is with return, not risk. D offers the highest expected return, 29%. For a risk neutral investor, $A = 0$, so $U = E(r)$.

4. The utilities are calculated below.

$$U(A) = .12 - (.5) (-2) (.29^2) = 0.2041$$
$$U(B) = .15 - (.5) (-2) (.35^2) = 0.2725$$
$$U(C) = .24 - (.5) (-2) (.38^2) = 0.3844$$
$$U(D) = .29 - (.5) (-2) (.44^2) = \mathbf{0.4836}$$

For a person with $A = -2$, the second part of the utility function becomes positive instead of negative. An investment with a higher standard deviation adds to the utility, or satisfaction, level. People who are risk lovers have negative risk aversion coefficients. They prefer to take on risk in the hope of earning higher returns.

5. The risk premium is 7.5%, so the required return on the investment equals the risk premium plus the risk-free rate: 7.5% + 4.0% = 11.5%. The value of any asset is the present value of its cash flows, $PV_0 = FV_n / (1+r)^n$. The value of the $24,000 to be received one year from today is ($24,000 / 1.115) = $21,524.66. Alternately, [($24,000 – P) / P] = .115; 0.115 (P) = $24,000 – P; 1.115 (P) = $24,000; P = $21,524.66.

6. a. The utility levels are calculated below.

$$U_1 = 12.9\% - (.5) * (1.5) * (18.6^2) = 10.31\%$$
$$U_2 = 12.9\% - (.5) * (3.5) * (18.6^2) = 6.85\%$$
$$U_3 = 12.9\% - (.5) * (6.0) * (18.6^2) = 2.52\%$$

   b. The certainty equivalent (CE) rate of return for investor 1 is 10.31%. This person would be indifferent between the risky investment in Ukrainian Egg Decorators and a risk-free investment that offered 10.31%. Similarly, investor 2 has a CE of 6.85% and investor 3 has a CE of 2.52%. As the level of risk aversion rises (as A gets bigger) the investors become more willing to accept a lower rate for certain than to take on a risky prospect that offers a higher, but uncertain, expected rate of return.

7. The Mean-Variance criterion states that investment 1 dominates investment 2 if investment 1 has an equal or higher mean return and an equal or lower variance of returns than investment 2, with at least one inequality holding. (Both the mean and the variance cannot be equal or the investor would be indifferent between the two investments.) The table below shows which investments are dominated by others, and which are efficient.

Investment	Expected Return	Standard Deviation of Returns	Inefficient?
A	5.30%	9.30%	yes, dominated by C
B	12.40%	11.40%	yes, dominated by C, D
C	14.63%	8.47%	no
D	37.47%	9.40%	no
E	7.90%	47.20%	yes, dominated by B, C, D
F	3.83%	1.25%	no

Therefore, the efficient set consists of investments C, D, and F.

8. Only investment T is preferred to Q by all risk averse investors because it has both a higher expected return and a lower standard deviation than Q. Investment R has both a lower expected return and a lower standard deviation, which are both unfavorable. Investment R would not be preferred to Q by any risk averse investor.

Investment S has a lower standard deviation, which is favorable, but it also has a lower expected return, which is unfavorable. Investment U has a higher expected return, which is favorable, but it also has a higher standard deviation, which is unfavorable. These two investments (S and U) could potentially be on the same indifference curve as Q if the tradeoffs between expected return and standard deviation are equally acceptable to an investor.

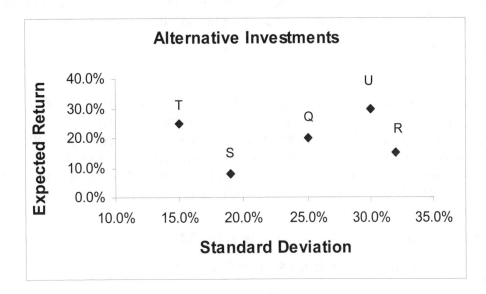

9. The expected return, $E(r_P)$, is the weighted average of the returns of the two securities: $E(r_P) = 0.7(12\%) + 0.3(5\%) = 9.9\%$. The portfolio's standard deviation is the weight in the risky asset times the standard deviation of the risky asset: $\sigma_P = 0.7(0.04)^{1/2} = 14.0\%$.

10. Since the return is a weighted average of the returns of the two assets, we can set the problem up as $8\% = y(13\%) + (1 - y)(4\%)$, where y is the proportion in the risky asset. Then rearranging we have $8\% = 13\%y + 4\% - 4\%y$. Next, $4\% = 9\%y$ so $y = 0.4444$ and $1 - y = 0.5556$. The investor should put 44.44% of the portfolio in the risky asset and 55.56% in the risk-free asset. To verify, $0.4444(13\%) + 0.5556(4\%) = 9.0\%$.

11. The standard deviation of the portfolio would be the standard deviation of the risky asset times the percentage of wealth invested in it, $y \times \sigma_p$, or $(.444)(14\%) = 6.22\%$.

12. Since the standard deviation of a portfolio is the percent of wealth invested in the risky asset times the standard deviation of the risky asset, the problem can be set up as $0.05 = y(0.14)$. Here, y is the proportion in the risky asset. Solving, $y = .3571$. or 35.71% in the risky asset. This means that the balance of the portfolio, or 62.49%, will be invested in the risk-free asset.

13. The required return is ($122 – 100) / $100 = 22%. Since the portfolio return is a weighted average of the return on the assets the problem can be set up as $.22 = y(.13) + (1 – y)(.04)$. Rearranging and solving, $.22 = .13y + .04 – .04y$. Therefore, $0.18 = 0.09y$. Thus $y = 2$ (200%) and $(1 – y) = –1$ (–100%). This suggests that we invest $200 in the risky asset. To do this we –$100 in the T-bill (we borrow $100 at the risk free rate). Confirming the expected return:

    $(2)(13\%) + (–1)(4\%) = 22\%$.

14. The slope is the return on the risky investment minus the return on the risk-free investment, divided by the standard deviation of the risky investment or (0.13 – 0.04) / 0.14 = 0.6429. Alternatively, we could use the particular portfolio formed by the investor by combining the risky asset with the risk-free asset, which has an expected return of 8% and a standard deviation of 6.22%. The slope is calculated as (.08 – .04) / .0622 = 0.6429. This makes sense because both the risky asset and the portfolio lie on the CAL.

    The intercept for the CAL is the risk-free rate, .04.

    The equation for the CAL is $E(r_C) = .04 + 0.6429 \sigma_C$.

15. The CAL will have a kink in it beyond point P because going beyond P means y > 1 and the investor is borrowing at the higher rate. The slope of the CAL in the borrowing portion is (0.13 – .09) / 0.14 = 0.2857. The reward-to-volatility ratio is lower than it was in the lending portion (0.6429) because the investor must pay the higher rate to borrow.

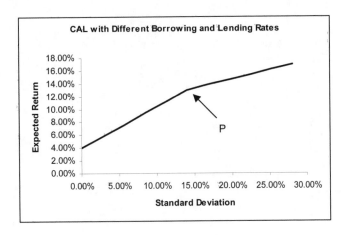

16. The expected return of the portfolio should be (–.3) (6%) + (1.3) (13%) = 15.1%.

17. The expected standard deviation of the portfolio should be (1.3) (14%) = 18.2%.

Chapter 7 Answers
Optimal Risky Portfolios

1. The expected returns are the probability-weighted returns from the table.

    $E(r_K) = 0.1(10\%) + 0.2(11\%) + 0.4(12\%) + 0.2(13\%) + 0.1(14\%) = 12\%$, or .12

    $E(r_L) = 0.1(9\%) + 0.2(8\%) + 0.4(7\%) + 0.2(6\%) + 0.1(9\%) = 7.4\%$, or .074

2. Using the expected average returns computed in the previous problem of (K = 12% and L = 7.4%) and the information from the table above we get:

    $\sigma_K = [0.1(10\% - 12\%)^2 + 0.2(11\% - 12\%)^2 + 0.4(12\% - 12\%)^2 + 0.2(13\% - 12\%)^2 +$
    $0.1(14\% - 12\%)^2]^{1/2} = 1.0954\%$, or .010954.

    $\sigma_L = [0.1(9\% - 7.4\%)^2 + 0.2(8\% - 7.4\%)^2 + 0.4(7\% - 7.4\%)^2 + 0.2(6\% - 7.4\%)^2 +$
    $0.1(9\% - 7.4\%)^2]^{1/2} = 1.0198\%$, or .–.010198.

3. To find the covariance, we use the probabilities and expected returns for each state and the average (expected) returns computed above, ($E(r_K) = 12\%$ and $E(r_L) = 7.4\%$).

    $Cov(r_K, r_L) = 0.1(.10 - .12)(.09 - .074) + 0.2(.11 - .12)(.08 - .074) +$
    $0.4(.12 - .12)(.07 - .074) + 0.2(.13 - .12)(.06 - .074) +$
    $0.1(.14 - .12)(.09 - .074) = -0.00004$

4. The correlation coefficient is the covariance between the securities divided by the product of their standard deviations, so $\rho_{K,L} = -0.00004 / [(.010954)(.010198)] = -0.3581$

5. The expected return to a portfolio invested 35% in K and 65% in L would be
    $E(R_P) = 0.35(12\%) + 0.65(7.4\%) = 9.01\%$

6. The standard deviation of the portfolio is the square root of its variance. The variance of a portfolio comprised of two assets (K and L) is $\sigma_P^2 = (w_K)^2 (\sigma_K^2) + (w_L)^2 (\sigma_L^2) + 2 (w_K) (w_L) (\sigma_K) (\sigma_L) \rho_{K,L}$.

    $\sigma_P = [(0.35)^2(.010954)^2 + (0.65)^2(.010198)^2 + 2(0.35)(0.65)(.010954)(1.00198)$
    $(-0.3581)]^{1/2} = 0.006359$, or 0.6359%. Note that the standard deviation of the portfolio is much less than either of the securities' standard deviations due to the negative correlations between the securities' returns.

7. The optimal weights in the global minimum variance portfolio can be expressed as:

$$w_K = \frac{\sigma_L^2 - Cov(r_K, r_L)}{\sigma_K^2 + \sigma_L^2 - [2Cov(r_K, r_L)]} \quad \text{and} \quad w_L = 1 - w_K$$

Substituting in the values that we previously calculated we get:

$w_K = [(.010198)^2 - (-0.00004)] / [(.010954)^2 + (.010198)^2 - (2)(-0.00004)] = 0.4737$

$w_L = 1 - 0.4737 = 0.5263$

8. Using the weights calculated for the global minimum variance portfolio and the expected returns on K and L, we get $E(R_G) = 0.4737(12\%) + 0.5263(7.4\%) = 9.58\%$.

9. $\sigma_G = [(0.4737)^2(.010954)^2 + (0.5263)^2(.010198)^2 + (2)(0.4737)(0.5263)(-0.3581)(1.0954)(1.0198)]^{1/2} = .005982$, or 0.5982%.

10. The covariance of the securities can be computed by multiplying the correlation coefficient of the securities by the product of their standard deviations, so $Cov(r_A, r_B) = (.6)(.22)(.29) = .03828$.

11. a. The slope of the optimal CAL is the return on the optimal risky portfolio minus the risk-free rate divided by the standard deviation of the optimal risky portfolio, or $(.11 - .04) / .20 = 0.35$.
    b. The risk-free asset plots as the y intercept, with a standard deviation of 0% and an expected return of 4%. Portfolio P plots farther out on the line, with a standard deviation of 20% and an expected return of 11%. The graph is shown below.
    c. Point C is 80% of the way up the line between r_f and P, since you are investing 80% in the risky portfolio.

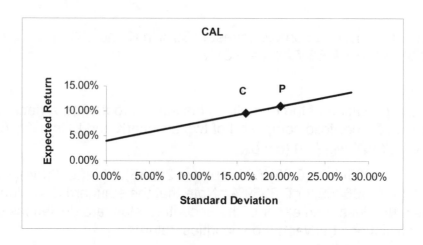

12. The expected return on portfolio O is
$E(r_O) = .23 \times 8\% + .77 \times 19\% = 16.47\%$

13. The expected return on the complete portfolio is
$E(r_C) = .34 \times 4.9\% + (1-.28) \times 16.47\% = 12.54\%$

14. The standard deviation of the complete portfolio is
$\sigma_C = (1-.34) \times 21\% = .66 \times 21\% = 13.86\%$

15. The weights of the risk-free asset, Fund A, and Fund B in the complete portfolio are calculated as shown in the table below.

Asset	Proportion in O	Weight in C
T-bills	0%	34.00%
Fund A	23%	$.23 \times 66\% = 15.18\%$
Fund B	77%	$.77 \times 66\% = 50.82\%$
		Total = 100%

Refer to the following information to answer questions 16 through 18 below.

Consider the following returns, variance, and correlations for stocks 1 through 4.

Stock	Weight	Return	Standard Deviation
1	0.10	10%	16%
2	0.20	11%	17%
3	0.40	12%	18%
4	0.30	13%	19%

Correlation Matrix

	1	2	3	4
1	1			
2	0.20	1		
3	0.40	0.60	1	
4	0.30	0.70	0.50	1

16. The return of the portfolio would be $E(r_p) = 0.1(10\%) + 0.2(11\%) + 0.4(12\%) + 0.2(13\%) = 10.6\%$,

17. The variance of the portfolio would be

$$(.1)^2(.16)^2 + (.2)^2(.17)^2 + (.4)^2(.18)^2 + (.3)^2(.19)^2 +$$

$$(2)(.1)(.2)(.16)(.17)(0.20) +$$

$$(2)(.1)(.4)(.16)(.18)(0.40) +$$

$$(2)(.1)(.3)(.16)(.19)(0.30) +$$

$$(2)(.2)(.4)(.17)(.18)(0.60) +$$

$$(2)(.2)(.3)(.17)(.19)(0.70) +$$

$$(2)(.4)(.3)(.18)(.19)(0.50) = 0.0235902$$

18. The standard deviation of the portfolio would be $(0.0235902)^{1/2} = 0.15359102$ (or) 15.36%.

Chapter 8 Answers
Index Models

1. The expected returns of each of the 450 securities must be calculated. In addition, the 450 variances around these returns must be calculated.

2. The number of covariances that must be calculated is $(n^2 - n) / 2 = (202{,}500 - 450) / 2 = 101{,}025$.

3. For a single-index model, 250 (equal to n) expected excess returns and 250 (also equal to n) sensitivity coefficients to the common macroeconomic factor must be estimated.

4. The expected return-beta relationship of the single index model is given by $E(R_i) = \alpha_i + \beta_i E(R_M)$. Since $\alpha_i = 0$, $E(R_i) = 5\% + 7\% = 12\%$, and $E(R_M) = 12\%$, we have $12\% = 0\% + 12\% * \beta_i$, so $\beta_i = 1.0$.

5. Beta can be found by using the equation $\sigma_P^2 / \sigma_M^2 = \beta^2$. Therefore, $\beta^2 = (0.22)^2 / (0.18)^2 = 1.494$ and $\beta = (1.494)^{1/2} = 1.222$.

6. Then standard deviation of security A can be calculated as $\sigma_A = [\beta_A^2 \sigma_m^2 + \sigma^2(e_A)]^{1/2}$. Therefore, $\sigma_A = [(.9)^2 (.24)^2 + (.12)^2]^{1/2} = .2417 = 24.71\%$.

7. The covariance can be estimated as $Cov(r_A, r_B) = \beta_A \beta_B \sigma_M^2$, or $(0.6)(1.4)(0.26)^2 = 0.05678$.

8. The variance of stock A equals $\beta_A^2 \sigma_M^2 + \sigma^2(e_A) = (0.60)^2 (0.26)^2 + (0.20)^2 = 0.064336$. So $\sigma_A = 0.064336^{(1/2)} = 25.36\%$. Likewise, the variance of stock B equals $\beta_B^2 \sigma_M^2 + \sigma^2(e_B) = (1.40)^2 (0.26)^2 + (0.10)^2 = 0.142496$, and $\sigma_B = 0.142496^{(1/2)} = 37.75\%$.

9. The systematic risk component of the variance for security A is given by $\beta_A^2 \sigma_M^2$, so A's systematic risk equals $(0.60)^2 (0.26)^2 = 0.0243$. The firm-specific risk is represented by $\sigma^2(e_A)$, which equals 0.0400. The sum of these two (0.0643) equals the total risk, or variance, of security A.

Likewise, the systematic risk component of B's variance equals $\beta_B^2\, \sigma_M^2$, or $(1.40)^2\, (0.26)^2 = 0.1325$. The firm-specific risk is represented by $\sigma^2(e_B)$, which equals 0.0100. The sum of these two (0.1425) equals the total risk, or variance, of security B.

10. The covariance between stock A and the market is $\beta_A\, \sigma_M^2$, so $Cov(r_A, r_M) = (0.60)(0.0676) = 0.0406$. The covariance between stock B and the market is $\beta_B\, \sigma_M^2$, so $Cov(r_B, r_M) = (1.40)(0.0676) = 0.0946$.

11. The correlation coefficient between stocks A and B equals is $(\beta_A\, \beta_B\, \sigma_M^2) / (\sigma_A\, \sigma_B)$, or $\rho_{A,B} = [(0.60)\,(1.40)\,(0.0676)] / [(.2536)\,(.3775)] = 0.5931$.

12. The Merrill Lynch adjusted beta equals (2/3) (sample beta) + (1/3) (1), so the adjusted beta is (2/3) (1.43) + (1/3) = 1.27.

13. Inserting the given values into the equation and solving, the estimate of beta will be $0.4 + 0.85(0.8) = 1.08$.

14. First, find the adjusted beta [adjusted beta = (2/3) (1.25) + (1/3) (1) = 1.167]. Then, use the adjusted beta and the information on the market rate and the risk free rate to find the return, $E(R_m) = 5\% + 1.167(12\% - 5\%) = 13.17\%$.

15. According to the model, the forecast beta = $.047 + 0.88(1.24) + 6.3(.053) - 0.4(0.74) = 1.1761$.

16. When security returns can be well approximated by normal distributions that are correlated across securities, it is said that the securities are *joint normally distributed*. This assumption alone implies that, at any one time, *security returns are driven by one or more common variables*. When more than one variable drives normally distributed security returns, these returns are said to have a *multivariate normal* distribution.

17. The optimal portfolio derived from the single-index model can be inferior to the full (Markowitz) covariance model when stocks with correlated residuals have *large alphas* and account for *a large fraction* of the portfolio. If many pairs of the stocks exhibit residual correlation, it is possible that a *multi-index model* would be better suited to portfolio construction and *analysis*.

Chapter 9 Answers
The Capital Asset Pricing Model

1. a. The equilibrium value of the market risk premium is the difference between its expected return and the risk-free rate, $E(r_M) - r_f$. According to the CAPM,

$$E(r_M - r_f) = \overline{A}\,\sigma_M^2 = 1.7 \times .17^2 = .0491.$$

   The expected rate of return on the market equals

   r_f + equilbrium market risk premium = 3.9% + 4.91% = 8.81%

   b. If the average investor has a risk aversion coefficient equal to 2.8, the equilibrium market risk premium will be 14.81% and the expected rate of return on the market equals 18.71%. It makes sense that the more risk averse investors are on average, the higher the expected return they would demand.

2. The CAPM states that the expected return on any security equals the risk-free rate plus the risk premium on the security. A security's risk premium equals the market risk premium (the expected return on the market minus the risk-free rate) times the beta of the security. Therefore, $E(R_i)$ = 3.5% + 1.63 (10.5 – 3.5) = 14.91%.

3. Alpha must be computed to answer this question. Alpha equals the actual expected return minus the theoretically correct (CAPM) return. A zero alpha represents a fairly priced security. If the alpha is nonzero, the security is mispriced. A positive alpha means the return on the security is too high relative to what it should be according to the CAPM, and therefore its price is too low – it is underpriced A negative alpha means the security is overpriced.

   For this stock, the CAPM indicates that the return should equal 3.5% + 1.25 (10.5% – 3.5%) = 12.25%. Since you actually expect a 12% return, alpha equals 12% – 12.25% = –0.25%. The negative alpha indicates that the security is overpriced. (Remember – prices and returns move in opposite directions. You expect to get only 12%, when you should be getting 12.25% for a security with a beta of 1.25; the lower return is caused by a price that is too high.)

4. The beta of a portfolio is a weighted average of the betas of the securities in the portfolio. A total of $1,000 is invested. The proportion in the first security is $550/$1,000 = 0.55. The proportion in the second security is $450/$1,000 = .45. Therefore, the beta of the portfolio is (0.55)(1.12) + (0.45)(0.86) = 1.003.

5. According to the CAPM, the return on the security should equal 4.5% + 1.1 (7.5% – 4.5%) = 7.8%. Alpha equals the return you actually expect minus the CAPM return, or 11% – [4.5% +1.1(7.5% – 4.5%)], which equals 3.2%.

6. Security A's excess return, or alpha, is expected to be 12.2% – [3.5% + 1.23(10.5% – 3.5%)] = 0.09%. Security B's excess return is expected to be 13.9% – [3.5% + 1.81(10.5% – 3.5%)] = –2.27%. Therefore, security A is a better buy since it is underpriced. Security B is overpriced.

7. Since alpha is assumed to be zero, the return on the security must equal the return specified by the CAPM. Therefore, inserting the known values into the CAPM equation means that 15% = [3.5% + β(10.5% – 3.5%)]. Rearranging the equation, 11.5% = β (7%), and β = 1.64.

8. If the security is fairly priced, the alpha is zero and the SML (CAPM) equation must hold. Inserting the known values we have 13% = [3.5% + 1.1($E(R_m)$ – 3.5%)]. Then 9.5% = $1.1E(R_m)$ – 3.85%, so 13.35% = $1.1E(R_m)$, and $E(R_m)$ = 12.136%.

9. Inserting values into the CAPM gives 12% = R_f + 1.27 (10.5% – R_f). Then 12% = R_f + 13.335% – $1.27R_f$, –1.335% = $-0.27R_f$, and R_f = 1.335% / 0.27 = 4.94%.

10. A security's beta equals its covariance divided by the variance of the market, so this security has a beta of 0.06 / 0.05 = 1.20.

11. Beta equals the covariance of the security divided by the variance of the market: .86 = $.05/\sigma_M^2$. So σ_M^2 = .05/.86 = 0.058.

12. a. The intercept of the SML is the risk-free rate, 4.5%.
    b. The slope of the SML is the risk premium on the market, 11% − 4.5% = 6.5%.
    c. The expected return on asset E equals 4.5% + 1.37 × 11% = 13.41%.
    d. The SML and points M and E are shown below.

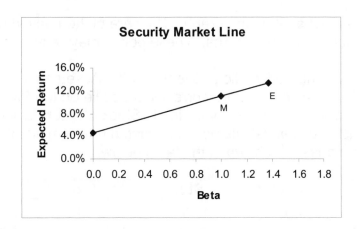

13. Long Beach Ladder should use the beta of the project, not the firm, to evaluate the project. According to the CAPM, the project's expected return should be
    E(r) = 5% + 2.0 × (12% − 5%) = 19%.
    At a discount rate of 19% the net present value of the project is
    $57,000 × PVIFA $_{5,19\%}$ −$175,000 = −$714.81, so the project should be rejected.
    [Calculator entries: The present value of the cash inflows is calculated as N = 5,
    I / Y = 19, PMT = 57,000, FV = 0, CPT PV → $174,285.19
    The NPV of the project is $174,285.19 − 175,000 = −$714.81]

14. a. The CAPM returns, based on the relationship $E(r_i) = r_f + B_i \times (E(r_M) - r_f)$, are shown in the table.

   b. The SML is shown below. The intercept is the risk-free rate, 6.1%, and the slope is $(E(r_M) - r_f)$, 14.6% − 6.1% = 8.5%. The CAPM expected returns lie on the SML.

   c. The assets are labeled on the graph. They are plotted based on their betas and their actual expected returns. These points may lie above, below, or on the SML.

   d. Assets that are underpriced lie above the SML. Assets that are overpriced lie below the SML. Assets that are correctly priced lie on the SML. Stocks 1 and 3 are underpriced. Stock 2 is overpriced. Stock 4 is correctly priced. The alpha for each stock equals its actual expected return minus its "fair", or CAPM return. The alphas are shown in the table below.

	Stock 1	Stock 2	Stock 3	Stock 4
Bi	−0.10	0.67	1.95	2.20
CAPM $E(r_i)$	5.25%	11.80%	22.68%	24.80%
Actual $E(r_i)$	6.29%	9.08%	27.24%	24.80%
Fairly Priced?	underpriced	overpriced	underpriced	correctly priced
alpha	2.23%	−1.61%	8.63%	0.00%

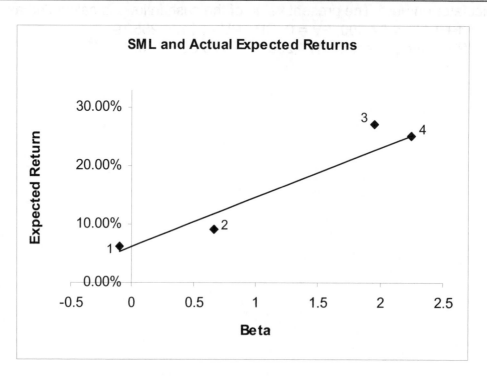

134

15. a. According to the CAPM, the expected return would equal
$E(r_i) = r_f + B_i \times (E(r_M) - r_f) = 4.30\% + 0.90 \times (13\% - 4.3\%) = 12.13\%$.
   b. Given this expected return, you would be willing to pay the present value of the perpetual dividends for the stock. Price = $6.00 / .1213 = $49.46.
   c. If the actual beta of the stock is 1.30, the required rate of return would be
$E(r_i) = r_f + B_i \times (E(r_M) - r_f) = 4.30\% + 1.30 \times (13\% - 4.3\%) = 15.61\%$. The most you should have paid for it is $6.00 / .1561 = $38.44. You would have paid $49.46 - 38.44 = $11.03 too much.

16. The simplifying assumptions that lead to the basic version of CAPM are:
   a. investors are price takers (the perfect competition assumption of microeconomics)
   b. all investors plan for an identical holding period
   c. investments are limited to publicly traded financial assets
   d. investors may borrow and lend at the risk-free rate
   e. there are no taxes or transactions costs
   f. all investors are rational mean-variance optimizers
   g. all investors analyze securities in the same way and have homogeneous expectations.

17. The Consumption CAPM (CCAPM) is built on the premise that in a lifetime consumption plan, investors must balance the allocation of wealth between today's consumption and investment that will support future consumption. Optimally, the utility value of an additional dollar of current consumption must equal that of future consumption that can be financed by that additional dollar of wealth. The attractiveness of the CCAPM is that it incorporates consumption hedging and potential changes in investment opportunities. Moreover, Jagannathan and Wang (2007) suggest that the CCAPM is more successful in explaining realized return than the CAPM.

Chapter 10 Answers
Arbitrage Pricing Theory and
Multifactor Models of Risk and Return

1. a. Arbitrage is the ability to earn a riskless profit by exploiting security mispricings. For example, if Alltel (AT) stock sells on the Philadelphia exchange for $54.23 per share and on the New York exchange for $54.24 per share there is an arbitrage opportunity. You can short sell one million shares of AT on the NYSE and get $54.24 million. Then buy one million shares on the Philadelphia exchange for $54.23 million and cover the short sale. Without taking any risk you will realize a profit of $10,000. This example ignores transactions costs, but the results would be similar if profitable arbitrage opportunities exist.

    b. A zero-investment portfolio is one for which investors do not use any of their own money. The example above would be a zero-investment portfolio because the investor uses the proceeds from the short sale in the overpriced market to cover the purchase of sales in the underpriced market.

    c. The APT says that if markets are in equilibrium no arbitrage opportunities should exist. Investors should not be able to form a zero-investment portfolio that will yield a riskless profit.

    d. Coefficients are called factor betas, factor loadings, or factor sensitivities.

2. To solve this problem, start by computing the returns to the factor for each portfolio using the relationship $E(r_P) = r_f + \beta_P F$. Once the factor returns are computed, the strategy should be to short sell the portfolio with the low return to the factor and buy the portfolio with the high return to the factor. In this case, the return to the factor for portfolio A would be $14\% = 5\% + 1.2F$. Therefore, $F = 7.50\%$ for portfolio A. For portfolio B it would be $9\% = 5\% + 0.7F$. So $F = 5.71\%$ for portfolio B. Therefore, short B and take a long position in A.

3. The portfolio variance is given by $\sigma_P^2 = B_P^2 \sigma_F^2 + \sigma^2(e_P)$. For well-diversified portfolios, $\sigma^2(e_P)$ (nonsystematic risk) approaches zero due to diversification effects. So a reasonable estimate of this portfolio's beta is its beta squared times the variance of returns on the factor portfolio. That is, a good approximation is that $\sigma_P^2 = (1.3)^2(.05) = .0845$.

4. As above, the portfolio variance is the beta squared times the variance of returns on the factor portfolio. Inserting the known values and rearranging we have $(.20)^2 = \beta^2(.17)^2$. Therefore, $\beta^2 = 1.384$ and $\beta = 1.17647$.

5. To preclude arbitrage opportunities, the law of one price must hold (both stocks must have the same return for the common factor). Therefore, set up the equations and using the information available for stock B, solve for the factor's return: 16% = 5% + (1.1)(F), so F = 10%. Then use the factor's return that you just computed to solve for the beta of stock A, where 12% = 5% + βF. Since F =10%, the beta of A = 7/10 = 0.70.

6. The return on the portfolio must equal the risk-free rate plus the sum of the products of each of the factor betas times the risk premium of that factor, or 12.2% = 5% + 1.2 (4%) + .6 (F2). So F2 = 4%.

7. The return on the portfolio must equal the risk-free rate plus the sum of the products of each of the factor betas times the risk premium of that factor, or E(r$_A$) = 4% + 0.92(2.3%) + 1.37(3.4%) = 10.774%.

8. The return to the portfolio must equal the risk-free rate plus the sum of the products of each of the factor betas times the risk premium to that factor. Inserting the known values, we have15% = r$_f$ + 1.0(5%) + 0.9(6%). Therefore, r$_F$ = 4.60%.

9. The return to the portfolio must equal the risk-free rate plus the sum of the products of each of the factor betas times the risk premium to that factor. Inserting the known values provides 14% = 6% + (0.8)(3%) + B2(4%). Therefore, B2 = 1.4.

10. The portfolio return would be an equally weighted average of the returns of the stocks assuming that the specified state of nature is realized, or E(r$_p$) = 0.5(18%) + 0.5(16%) = 17%.

11. The nonsystematic standard deviation of an equally weighted portfolio can be calculated as follows (the last term is the average nonsystematic variance)

$$\sigma^2(e_p) = \frac{1}{n}\overline{\sigma^2(e_i)} = \frac{1}{60}(22)^2 = 8.067, \quad \sigma(e_p) = \sqrt{8.067} = 2.84\%$$

The nonsystematic standard deviation of the portfolio is smaller than the average nonsystematic standard deviation of the securities and will approach zero as the number of securities increases.

12. a. The risk premium on the first factor is 11% − 5.2% = 5.8%.
    b. The risk premium on the second factor is 17% − 5.2% = 11.8%.
    c. The risk premium on portfolio Z due to its exposure to the first factor equals
       1.1 x 5.8 = 6.38%.
    d. The risk premium on portfolio Z due to its exposure to the second factor equals
       0.45 x 11.8% = 5.31%.
    e. The total risk premium on portfolio Z equals 6.38% + 5.31% = 11.69%
    f. The total expected return on portfolio Z equals 11.69% + 5.2% = 16.89%.

13. Chen, Roll, and Ross chose macroeconomic factors as relevant for pricing
    securities. The five factors selected were
    - the % change in industrial production (IP)
    - the % change in expected inflation (EI)
    - the % change in unanticipated inflation (UI)
    - the excess return of long-term corporate bonds over long-term government
      bonds (CG)
    - the excess return o long-term government bonds over T-bills (GB)

14. Fama and French used a three factor model that included
    - the return on a market index (RM)
    - the return on a portfolio of small cap stocks minus the return on a portfolio of
      large cap stocks (SMB)
    - the return on a portfolio of stocks of firms with high book-to-market value
      ratios minus the return on a portfolio of stocks of firms with low book-to-market
      ratios (HML)

15. a. The expected return on the stock would be
       4.8% + 1.7(2.0%) + 0.9(10.5%) = 17.65%.
    b. The correct expected return would be
       4.8% + 1.7(3.5%) + 0.9(9.0%) = 18.85%
    c. If you required a return of 17.65% on the stock, you required too little and would
       have been willing to pay too much. You would have overpriced the stock.

16. The three key propositions underlying Ross's APT are: (1) security returns can be
    described by a factor model, (2) there are sufficient securities to diversify away
    idiosyncratic risk, and (3) well-functioning securities markets do not allow for the
    persistence of arbitrage opportunities.

17. You can distinguish a multi-factor CAPM model from a multi-factor by examining
    because <u>CAPM</u> risk factors will be inherited from sources of risk that a broad group
    of investors considers important enough to hedge. However, <u>APT</u> is silent on
    where to look for priced risk factors.

Chapter 11 Answers
The Efficient Market Hypothesis

1. If stock prices follow a random walk, then changes in the prices should be unpredictable in direction and magnitude. Submartingales differ from a random walk in that the expected price change is positive (a random walk on a trend). New information about a firm will cause a change so that the price accurately reflects the true value of the firm.

2. Technical analysis is the search for recurrent and predictable patterns in security returns. Therefore, technical analysis involves the use of both charting and quantitative approaches to examine the past behavior and trends of security prices and using that information to attempt to predict the future.

3. Fundamental analysis is the use of fundamentals such as earnings and dividend prospects of the firm, expectations of future interest rates, and estimated risk of the firm to determine security prices. The goal is to estimate future cash flows and to find their present value to determine the appropriate market price.

4. The weak form of the EMH asserts that all historical information such as past prices, volume, short interest, and returns are already embedded in current prices. If markets are weak-form efficient, studying past prices and trends will not allow you to develop a trading rule that will consistently outperform the market as a whole. Therefore, if markets are weak-form efficient, technical analysis is useless.

5. The semistrong form of the EMH asserts that all publicly available information such as historical information, information of the firm's product lines, management quality, financial statements, trends in the industry, and information about competitors is already embedded in current security prices. Therefore, if markets are semistrong-form efficient, fundamental analysis is not useful in selecting securities that will consistently outperform the market.

6. The strong form of the EMH asserts that all information, including information only available to insiders, is already incorporated into security prices. It suggests that nobody, including those with inside information, could consistently select securities that would outperform the market. While this seems extreme, SEC Rule 10-b5 sets limits on and requires disclosure of insiders' trades. Violation of the rules may lead to prosecution, fines, and prison time for violators.

7. The types of efficiency are cumulative because each form has the previous form's data included as a subset. The semi-strong form definition of information includes the weak form data (prices, trading volume, etc.) and adds other publicly available information. The strong form definition of information includes the historical (weak form) data, the public (semi-strong form) data, and adds inside information.

8. Technical analysts think that prices respond slowly to changes in fundamental factors that influence supply and demand for a firm's stock. Investors who believe in the EMH think that prices respond very quickly to new information. They think that by the time an individual investor gets new information and can act on it, it is already incorporated in the stock's price.
   Also, technical analysts believe that patterns in stock prices are identifiable and can be used to earn superior profits. Those who think markets are efficient believe that stock price changes follow a random walk. Therefore they say that investors cannot profit from examining price patterns because future prices cannot be predicted.

9. Small investors don't have the funds or the resources necessary to benefit from superior fundamental analysis. Suppose a small investor has a portfolio of $50,000. If (s)he is able to use fundamental analysis to increase profits by 2% above what (s)he would have earned, (s)he brings in only $1,000 extra. It is unlikely that this is a satisfying payoff for the effort expended. Mutual fund managers and ETF managers can take advantage of large portfolio sizes and the analytical resources that are available to them. They can perform analyses much more efficiently than individuals. As long as the benefits of using mutual funds and ETFs outweigh the costs, individual investors are better off using them.

10. The market for Google stock is likely to be much more efficient. There is more information available in developed markets. The information can be verified by institutional investors that follow the firm and analyze its performance and prospects. Market efficiency hinges on the availability and accuracy of information and its incorporation into the stock's price.

11. When security returns do not conform to expectations based on the CAPM an anomaly has occurred. If markets are efficient and assets are properly priced, anomalies should not exist. Once they are discovered, investors would act quickly to take advantage of them and the anomalies should disappear. Several anomalies have been documented in the literature. For example:
    a. the P/E effect – Basu found that portfolios containing low P/E ratio stocks tended to have higher returns than portfolios containing high P/E ratio stocks with similar risk.
    b. the small-firm effect – Banz found that portfolios of small firms' stocks tended to have higher returns than portfolios of larger firms' stocks with similar risk.
    c. the neglected-firm effect – Arbel found that stocks that were followed by fewer analysts tended to have higher returns than stocks that were more widely followed.
    d. the book-to-market effect – Fama and French found that portfolios of firms with high book-to-market ratios tended to have higher returns than firms with low book-to-market ratios.
    e. the reversal effect – DeBondt and Thaler found that stocks that performed poorly in the past tended to perform well in future periods and that firms that had performed very well in the past tended to perform poorly in the future. This helps explain the contrarian investment philosophy.

12. The magnitude issue focuses on the idea that, for very large portfolios, very small increases in performance can provide large dollar value payoffs, but these payoffs are usually statistically insignificant in percentage terms. This happens because securities markets tend to be very volatile.

    The selection bias issue refers to the fact that when fund managers' performances are evaluated, a large portion of the sample is automatically omitted. The funds that have performed poorly, for example, may have gone out of existence. The funds that remain for analysis are the survivors, so there is a bias present even before the analysis begins.

    The lucky event issue reflects the fact that, even in efficient markets, there is a distribution of potential outcomes that includes extreme outcomes. One cannot automatically assume that superior performance is the result of superior skill. It may be the result of random occurrences.

13. To answer the question you need to compute the expected return using the CAPM and then the abnormal return (AR). The AR is the realized return minus the expected return from CAPM. The CAPM predicts an expected return of 5% + 1.4(11%-5%) = 13.4%. So the AR = 16% – 13.4% = +2.6%. A positive abnormal return suggests that there was firm-specific good news.

14. To answer the question you need to compute the expected return using the CAPM and then the abnormal return (AR). The AR is the realized return minus the expected return from CAPM. Here, AR = 14% – (4% + 1.6 (12% – 4%)) = –2.8%. The negative abnormal return would suggest that the market viewed the announcement of a 3% sales increase as bad news. We can infer that the consensus growth for same store sales must have been greater the 3% growth that AMS realized. Rather than the absolute levels, the market evaluates announcements relative to the expectations investors and analysts held prior to the announcements.

15. To answer the question you need to compute the expected return using the CAPM and then the abnormal return (AR) for each of the days. The AR is the realized return minus the expected return from CAPM. Here it would be AR = 12% – (3.5% + 0.7 (10.5% – 3.5%)) = +3.6% for the day before yesterday and AR = 8.4% – (3.5% + 0.7 (10.5% – 3.5%)) = 0.0% for yesterday. This is an unusual situation but if the market were to react before the announcement, it may suggest that there was a leakage of information about the deal or insiders traded heavily on that day.

16. Studies of the stock price response to dividend announcements by Patel and Wolfson (1984) reveal that stock prices react <u>on the day that the news becomes public</u>. Moreover, Busse and Green's (2002) research suggests that the stock price of firms mentioned on CNBC's "Morining" or "Midday Call" segments react to positive news within <u>5 minutes</u> and react to negative news within <u>12 minutes</u>. This evidence <u>supports</u> the contention that stock prices react quickly to news.

17. Studies of the earnings announcements reveal that firms with positive earnings surprises <u>react </u>positively while firms with negative earnings <u>react negatively</u>. In both cases, there is <u>immediate</u> reaction to the news. However, the reaction <u>is not confined to the announcement day</u>. Firms with positive surprises <u>continue to drift higher for several months</u> while firms with negative surprises <u>continue to drift lower for several months</u>.

Chapter 12 Answers
Behavioral Finance and Technical Analysis

1. Behavioral finance is the study of how people actually behave instead of how rational investors should behave. Several information-processing errors have been documented in the literature such as forecasting errors, overconfidence, conservatism, sample size neglect and representativeness. Additionally, several behavioral biases have been documented. These biases suggest that investors are predisposed to react in certain ways rather than acting as rational mean-variance optimizers. Some of these biases include framing, mental accounting, and regret avoidance.

2. The efficient markets hypothesis (EMH) states that prices quickly and accurately reflect all relevant information that is available regarding the values of securities. If this is true, then technical analysis tools such as trading rules will not work because by the time a user can implement them the profit opportunity will have passed. The price of the stock will have risen or fallen so fast that the investor could not take advantage of it.

   Technical analysts believe that there are times when the market is not so efficient, and that prices may adjust slowly to new information. That gives the investor a chance to look for trends that offer potential profits and take action in time to benefit from the opportunity.

3. Henry is using mental accounting by separating his portfolio into several accounts rather than viewing it on an overall basis.

   It is more appropriate to view the entire portfolio as a whole. In this case, Henry could resolve his liquidity crisis by using the college funds so the family doesn't lose its home, which may lead to worse consequences than his children having to borrow money or work more themselves to pay for college. The home is also a part of Henry's portfolio and he may lose much or all of its value if the bank seizes it.

4. Aunt Alma is showing signs of forecasting error, an information processing problem. She is overemphasizing the most recent pattern in dividends and ignoring the years before the most recent ones. There may be no particular reason to assume that the irregular weather patterns will recur and there may be a high probability that the growth in dividends will resume.

5. Ed is experiencing overconfidence and sample size neglect and representativeness. His overconfidence is causing him to overestimate his abilities based on only the most recent two months. Some questions to ask Ed would be how long he has been investing, what his returns have been for the entire time, what changes he made two months ago, and what caused him to make the changes.

   As for sample size and representativeness, the two-month sample period is too brief to generalize the results and he may be talking about a portion of his overall portfolio rather than the whole thing. The securities he chose as investments might experience reversals in the near future.

6. A conventional utility function is concave over its entire range. This represents an investor whose satisfaction level will always rise as wealth rises, but satisfaction will rise at a decreasing rate.

   The utility function suggested by prospect theory reflects the idea that the investor has different attitudes toward changes in wealth, depending on whether the change is an increase or a decrease from the current level. Increases in wealth are viewed in a way similar to conventional utility theory. But for decreases in wealth, the utility curve is convex. This means that satisfactions drops rapidly at first as wealth is reduced. Investors tend to exhibit loss aversion in this range. As wealth keeps falling, satisfaction also falls, but at a much slower rate.

   An implication for investors is that they will evaluate investments relative to their current level of wealth. As their wealth shifts, they may take on riskier investments to try to stay in the concave portion of the curve (experience gains) and stay away from the convex portion (avoid losses).

7. The amount of the premium or the discount is

   $$\frac{\text{Price}-\text{NAV}}{\text{NAV}} = \frac{\alpha-\varepsilon}{\delta+\varepsilon-\alpha} = \frac{.02-.028}{.04+.028-.02} = -.1667 \text{, or a discount of } 16.67\%$$

   The fund may be trading at a discount because the expense ratio is higher than the risk-adjusted abnormal return. If the managers can reduce expenses and/or earn higher abnormal returns, the situation may reverse.

8. Given the initial values, the fair price for Round Barn is the present value of the growing perpetuity of dividends: $3.25 / (.11 − .06) = $65.00. When the growth rate is revised downward, the new price will be less: $3.25 / (.11 − .052) = $56.03. This is a result of rational evaluation on the part of shareholders. The stock's value is sensitive to the inputs used to determine it.

9. The Dow theory is based on the idea that there are three processes at work in the stock market. There is a primary trend, which is the long-term movement of prices. The primary trend may last from several months to several years. A secondary trend also occurs, which reflects short-term deviations of prices from an underlying trend line. The deviations are eliminated by corrections. A tertiary, or minor, trend results from daily fluctuations in prices and has little significance.

    Two variations of the Dow theory are the Elliott wave theory and the Kondratieff wave theory. According to the Elliott wave theory, stock prices follow long-term and short-term wave patterns. By interpreting the waves, an investment analyst can predict broad stock price movements. Kondratieff waves are caused by macroeconomic changes and follow a 48 to 60-year pattern.

10. Market breadth is an indication of whether price movements are widespread or relatively isolated. A broad market is one in which the price movements of a large number of stocks are influencing the market index. A narrow market occurs when the price movements of a small number of stocks are dominating the index value and causing its change.

    Financial analysts calculate the cumulative breadth of the market based on net advances and declines. They watch the direction of the cumulative breadth or a moving average of it to try to discover implied market trends.

11. The trin ratio is calculated by the equation

$$\text{trin} = \frac{\text{Number Advancing / Number Declining}}{\text{Volume Advancing / Volume Declining}}$$

    The ratio equals $\dfrac{8,511 / 4,214}{2,441,578 / 1,840,742} = 1.52$ on October 1 (bearish) and

    $\dfrac{8,785 / 10,861}{3,517,846 / 845,622} = 0.19$ on February 1 (bullish).

    A trin ratio above 1 is considered bearish and below 1 is considered bullish.

12. The confidence index is a guide to investors' market perceptions. It is based on the notion that trends that result from trading in the bond market precede similar trends in the stock market.

To calculate the index, divide the average yield on 10 top-rated corporate bonds by the average yield on 10 intermediate-grade corporate bonds. Since the top-rated bonds will offer lower yields than the intermediate-grade bonds, the confidence index will always be less than 1.

When economic conditions are weak, bond traders will require more of a premium on the top-rated debt relative to the intermediate-grade debt. The result will be a lower confidence index. When economic conditions are stronger, the size of the premium will shrink and the confidence index will move closer to 1.

13. The put/call ratio equals 202/259 = 0.78. A put/call ratio above the typical level of 65% is open to interpretation. Puts are purchased in anticipation of falling prices so some investors consider an increased put/call ratio bearish. These investors would be likely to sell when the ratio is 0.78. Others, called contrarians, believe that an increase in the put/call ratio indicates that the market is undervalued and that it would be a good time to buy. They expect that prices would rise soon to get to proper valuation levels.

14. Data mining is the tendency to identify patterns where they don't actually exist in the data. For example, it is easy to look at a graph of stock prices over the past year and formulate trading rules that would have worked to generate excess profits. It's much harder to generate successful trading rules before you know what the stock price is going to do. It is also unlikely that trading rules generated based on past observations will be successful for future investments.

15. The solid line on the graph represents the weekly closing prices. The calculations for the 4-week moving average are shown in the table below the graph. The dashed line on the graph represents the moving average, which is smoother than the original data. The buy (B) and sell (S) signals are shown with the arrows. If you had followed the buy and sell signals, it would appear to have been a profitable strategy. However, transactions costs may have caused your net profit to disappear or even be negative.

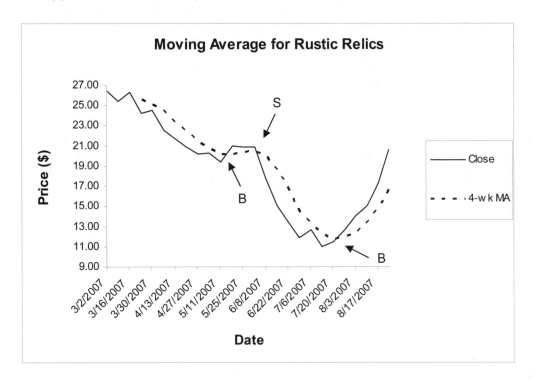

Date	Close	4 week Moving Average	Calculations for Moving Average
2-Mar-07	26.37		
9-Mar-07	25.43		
16-Mar-07	26.32		
23-Mar-07	24.23	25.59	=(26.37+25.43+26.32+24.23)/4
30-Mar-07	24.53	25.13	=(25.43+26.32+24.23+24.53)/4
6-Apr-07	22.53	24.40	=(26.32+24.23+24.53+22.53)/4
13-Apr-07	21.65	23.24	=(24.23+24.53+22.53+21.65)/4
20-Apr-07	20.90	22.40	=(24.53+22.53+21.65+20.90)/4
. . .	. . .	. . .	. . .
3-Aug-07	14.07	12.29	. . .
10-Aug-07	15.00	13.30	. . .
17-Aug-07	17.31	14.75	. . .
24-Aug-07	20.62	16.75	=(14.07+15.00+17.31+20.62)/4

16. Examples of violations to the Law of One Price for financial assets include Siamese twin companies, equity carve-outs, and closed-end funds. Siamese twin companies have been found to trade at prices that would violate the Law of One Price. For example Royal Dutch Petroleum and Shell Transport merged and the cash flows were split 60/40 which would imply a relative valuation of 60/40 = 1.5. However, the actual ratio has deviated substantially from parity and remained at non-parity levels for a substantial period. Equity carve-outs show similar parity violations. 3coms spin-off of palm is a prime example. Owners of 3com were entitled to 1.5 shares of palm. Since 3com was a profitable company, 3com shares should have been worth at least 1.5 times the value of palm. However, palm shares actually sold for more than 3coms share at the IPO. Finally, closed-end funds generally trade at discounts and premiums to NAV.

17. Behavioral biases would matter for stock prices if rational arbitrageurs could fully exploit the mistakes of behavioral investors. However, in practice, several factors limit the ability to exploit mispricings such as fundamental risk, implementation costs, and model risk.

Chapter 13 Answers
Empirical Evidence on Security Returns

1. The expected return beta relationship states that the expected return on security i is $E(r_i) = r_f + \beta_i ([E(r_M) - r_f]$. The CAPM relationship is based on an observable, ex ante market index return, $E(r_M)$ and β_i equals $Cov(r_i, r_M) / \sigma_M^2$.

2. The three basic steps used to test CAPM were: (1) establishing sample data, (2) estimating the security characteristic line (SCL), and (3) estimating the security market line (SML).

3. To estimate the security characteristic line (SCL) for each stock i, you would run the first-pass regression: $r_{it} - r_{ft} = a_i + b_i (r_{Mt} - r_{ft}) + e_{it}$. The subscript t denotes the time period. Typically, 5 years of monthly data are used, for a total of 60 observations. In the regression results the b_i coefficient is the estimate of the stock's beta.

4. To estimate the Security Market Line (SML), you would do a second-pass regression for each of the i securities that uses the estimate of the security's beta coefficient from the first pass regression. In this regression b_i is the independent variable and the form of the equation is $\overline{r_i - r_f} = \gamma_0 + \gamma_1 b_i$. If the CAPM is valid $\gamma_0 = 0$ and $\gamma_1 = \cdot \overline{r_i - r_f}$

   An alternative is to use a second-pass regression based on the equation $\overline{r_i - r_f} = \gamma_0 + \gamma_1 b_i + \gamma_2 \sigma^2(e_i)$. If this equation is used, the results should include $\gamma_0 = 0$, $\gamma_1 = \cdot \overline{r_i - r_f}$, and $\gamma_2 = 0$. That would imply that the security's expected return is base only on systematic risk, as measured by its beta.

5. Early tests of CAPM by Lintner (1965) and Miller and Scholes (1972) resulted in an estimated SML that was too flat (γ_1 was too small) and an intercept that was too high ($\gamma_0 > 0$).

6. Tests of CAPM have provided mixed evidence. The results can be summarized as:
   - Expected rates of return are linear and increase with beta, the measure of systematic risk. This supports the CAPM.
   - Expected rates of return are not affected by nonsystematic risk. This supports the CAPM.
   - The single-variable expected return-beta relationship is not fully consistent with empirical observations. This contradicts the CAPM.

7. While Roll had several criticisms of the CAPM, his claim that it is not testable arises primarily from the fact that the theory calls for the use of the expected return on the market portfolio. However, the true market portfolio cannot be observed nor its expected return estimated because it contains all assets. Therefore, CAPM cannot be tested. If the results of a CAPM test are negative, it may be due to a poor proxy for the market portfolio. If they are positive, they aren't valid because there is no guarantee that a good market proxy was used.

8. If the independent (right-hand-side) variable in a regression equation is measured with error it will lead to biased estimates of the regression coefficients. In the case of the CAPM, beta is measured with error because the true market portfolio cannot be observed. The result is that the regression's slope coefficient is biased downward and the intercept is biased upward. This is exactly what the test results showed - intercept γ_0 was higher than would be predicted by the CAPM and slope γ_1 was lower.

9. Human capital is a significant asset that is not traded. Therefore, it is not included in any market index that may be used as a proxy for the market portfolio. Mayers (1972) suggested the addition of a variable to the CAPM to measure the value of future wages and other forms of compensation. This variable would capture the portion of investors' wealth that will be generated during their careers. The diversification effects due to human capital are important to investors for two reasons:
   - they make up a substantial portion of investors' portfolios
   - the changes in wealth due to changes in human capital are likely to have low correlations with other assets' returns, so they offer diversification benefits.

10. Heaton and Lucas (2000) investigated the holdings of non-traded businesses in investors' portfolios because they represent a missing part of the proxies typically used for the market portfolio in the traditional CAPM. Their sample included U.S. households that had net worth over $10,000 and at least $500 of stock holdings in 1995. They looked at portfolio shares by age and net worth.
The main findings of the study were that:
- 19.8 million households met the criteria; this constitutes about 15% of the population of the U.S.
- about 10% of the sample had net worth over $1 million
- about 22% of the sample were over age 65
- the households whose members were over 65 held less wealth than those whose members were under 65
- for households whose members were under age 65 and with a net worth over $1 million, the median proprietary business ownership was 4.6% and the average was 18.1% of total wealth
- older households allocated a higher percent of their wealth to stock
- there was a highly significant negative relationship between the proportion of private business held as a part of total wealth and the proportion of stock held relative to total assets and to financial assets
- the less risk averse an investor perceived himself to be, the greater the proportion of stock he held in his portfolio

11. Chen, Roll, and Ross (1986) used a multifactor model that included the following variables in a linear regression: (1) the growth rate in industrial production (IP), (2) changes in expected inflation as measured by changes in T-bill interest rates (EI), (3) unexpected inflation, which was measured as the difference between actual and expected inflation (UI), (4) unexpected changes in risk premiums as measured by the difference between the returns on corporate Baa-rated bonds and long-term government bonds (CG), and (5) unexpected changes in the term premium as measured by the difference between the returns on long- and short-term government bonds (GB). The form of the first-pass regression equation was

$$R = a + B_M r_M + B_{IP} IP + B_{UI} UI + B_{CG} CG + B_{GB} GB + e$$

After obtaining the factor betas, they ran a second-pass regression based on

$$R = \gamma_0 + \gamma_M \beta_M + \gamma_{IP} \beta_{IP} + \gamma_{EI} \beta_{EI} + \gamma_{UI} \beta_{UI} + \gamma_{CG} \beta_{CG} + \gamma_{GB} \beta_{GB} + e$$

In this equation, each gamma coefficient estimated the risk premiums for the corresponding factor.

12. Fama and French (2000) used a three factor model that included the market index as well as firm size and book value to market value ratios. The HML (high minus low) factor captures the difference in book-to-market ratios and the SMB (small minus big) factor capturers the difference in size. The Fama-French model is

$$E(R_i) - r_f = a_i + b_i [E(r_m) - r_f] + s_i E(SMB) + h_i (HML).$$

The b_i, s_i, and h_i coefficients represent the sensitivity of the stock to the three factors.

13. Davis, Fama, and French (2000) sorted the firms in their sample by market capitalization and by book-to-market value ratio. The size premium SMB equaled the returns on the smallest third of the firms minus the returns on the largest third of the firms. The HML variable was constructed in a similar way.

14. Petkova and Zhang (2005) defined the state of the economy as a peak during periods with the 10% lowest risk premiums and as a trough during the 10% highest premiums. This confirmed the idea that beta tends to be counter-cyclical. In good economic times the betas of value stocks tend to be less than the betas of growth stocks. In bad economic times the opposite is true.

15. Survivorship bias occurs when only the performances of surviving funds are compared to an index to assess performance. This occurs because some companies regularly shut down funds that do not perform well. This act effectively buries their performance record. Therefore, when surviving funds are compared to an index, the performance looks better than it should since at least some of the poor-performing funds are not included in the comparison.

16. Early tests of the Consumption CAPM (CCAPM) found that CCAPM did not outperform the traditional CAPM. One challenge faced by early tests was that they used consumption data directly rather than returns on consumption tracking portfolios. Moreover, consumption data is collected less frequently and with substantial error.

17. Jagannathan and Wang (2006) tested the CCAPM by focusing on fourth quarter consumption and employing a consumption-mimicking portfolio. They find that annual consumption growth measured by comparing fourth quarter data in successive years is substantially better than the other intervals in explaining portfolio returns. The novel results are that the Fama-French factors are associated with consumption betas as well as excess returns. Moreover, a high book-to-market ratio is associated with a higher consumption beta, and firm size is inversely related to consumption beta. Thus, the explanatory power of the Fama-French factors may reflect differing consumption risk for those portfolios. Finally, the CCAPM explains returns even better than the Fama-Freench 3-factor model.

Chapter 14 Answers
Bond Prices and Yields

1. The default spread is the difference in yield on the risky bond and that of a Treasury of equal maturity. In this case, the default spread for California Pizza Kitchen is 6.7% – 4.7% = 2.0%. For Microsoft it is 7.9% – 5.7% = 2.2%.

2. The answers and the calculations are shown below.

Time	Inflation in Year Just Ended	Par Value	Coupon Payment	Principal Repayment	Total Payment	Nominal Return	Real Return
0		$1,000.00					
1	3.20%	$1,032.00	$47.47		$47.47	7.95%	4.60%
2	2.10%	$1,053.67	$48.47	$1,053.67	$1,102.14	6.80%	4.60%

Inflation rates and the coupon rate (4.6%) are given in the problem.
Par value year 1 = $1,000 × 1.032 = $1,032.00
Par value year 2 = $1,032 × 1.021 = $1,053.67
Coupon payment year 1 = .046 × $1,032.00 = $47.47
Coupon payment year 2 = .046 × $1,053.67 = $48.47
Principal Repayment occurs at maturity and is based on the par value at that time.
Total payment = coupon payment + principal repayment for each year
Nominal return year 1 = ($47.47 + 1,032.00 – 1,000) / $1,000 = 7.95%
Nominal return year 2 = ($48.47 + 1,053.67 – 1,032) / $1,032 = 6.80%
Real return year 1 = (1.0795 / 1.032) – 1 = 4.60%
Real return year 2 = (1.068 / 1.021) – 1 = 4.60%

3. A financial calculator comes in handy for bond problems. The keys that you use will be future value (FV), present value (PV), payment PMT, number of periods (N), and periodic interest rate (I/Y). In general, FV is the bond's face (par) value, PV is its current market price, PMT is the coupon payment (coupon rate times par), N is the number of periods until maturity, and I/Y is the yield to maturity. Enter the known values and compute the unknown.

    Given: FV = 1000, PMT = 72.5, n = 6, I/Y = 9.43. Compute PV ⇒ –903.45.

    [Note that the answer for PV is negative. (On some calculators this will not happen, but for most financial calculators it will.) What the calculator is assuming is that you need to have an outflow of $903.45 today to receive the PMT inflows and the FV at maturity. You could enter both FV and PMT as negative numbers and get a positive PV. Just be sure that FV and PMT always have the same sign. It is probably easiest to enter them as positive numbers and understand the interpretation of the negative result.]

4. For semi-annual coupon bonds, divide the annual coupon payment by two to get the PMT, multiply the number of years to maturity by two to get the number of periods (N), and divide the YTM by two to get I/Y.

   Given: FV = 1000, PMT = 55, n = 10, I/Y = 5. Compute PV $\Rightarrow$ –$1,038.61

5. Given: FV = 1000, PMT = 100, n = 5, PV = –889. Compute I/Y $\Rightarrow$ 13.17%

   [Note: If your calculator gives you an error message, recall your entries to be sure that FV and PMT have the same sign and PV has the opposite sign. See the interpretation of this in the answer to problem 2.]

6. Current yield (CY) is the annual interest divided by current price. Therefore, given: FV = 1000, n = 8, PMT = 90, I/Y = 10.5. Compute PV $\Rightarrow$ –921.41. Therefore, CY is $90 / $921.41 = 9.77%.

7. With zeroes, the PMT = 0. Therefore, $1,000/(1.09)^4 = $708.43, or given: FV = 1,000, PMT = 0, I/Y = 9, N = 4. Compute PV $\Rightarrow$ 708.43.

8. Start by computing the price that you paid for the bond. Given: FV = $1,000, I/Y = 11, PMT = 0, N = 12. Compute PV $\Rightarrow$ 285.84.
   Next compute the price for which you sold the bond. Given: FV = $1,000, I/Y = 12, PMT = 0, N = 11. Compute PV $\Rightarrow$ 287.48.
   The HPR = (287.48 – 285.84) / 285.84 = 0.57%

9. The price of the bond is 108% × $1,000 = $1,080. The bond accrues interest at a rate of (.12/12) × $1,000 = $10.00 per month. Since 2 months have passed since the last interest payment was made, 2 × $10 = $20 of interest has accrued. The invoice price of the bond will equal the market price plus the accrued interest, or $1,080 + $20, for a total invoice price of $1,100.

10. The effective annual yield (EAY) is (1 + the holding period return) raised to the number of compounding periods in one year, minus 1. Since you are buying it for $9,900 and will get $10,000 when it matures in one month, you will earn $100 in interest. The HPR = $100/$9,900 = 0.0101. Therefore, the EAY = $(1 + .0101)^{12}$ – 1 = 12.82%.

11. The conversion value is the number of shares times the price per share, or (31 shares) ($32/share) = $992.00.

12. The conversion premium is the market price minus the conversion value, or $995 – $992 = $3.

13. With a callable bond, the FV should be the call price and N should be the number of periods until the bond is callable. Given: YTC = FV = 1070, N = 10, PMT = 50, PV = –1,100. Compute I/Y $\Rightarrow$ 4.32% (semiannual), or (4.32) (2) = 8.64% annual.

14. Start by computing both prices.
Purchase price = Given: FV = 1000, PMT = 100, n = 8, I/Y = 9.
Compute PV $\Rightarrow$ 1055.35.
Sale price = Given: FV = 1000, PMT = 100, n = 7, I/Y = 8.
Compute PV $\Rightarrow$ 1104.13.
The interest received was (.10)($1,000) = $100.
The HPR is the capital gain plus the interest received divided by the purchase price, or HPR = (1104.13 – 1055.35 + 100) / 1055.35 = 14.10%.

15. The time line of the cash flows and the interest rates looks like the one below.

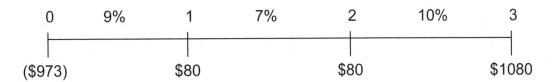

There is nothing to reinvest until the first coupon payment is received at time 1, so the 9% interest rate from time 0 to time 1 is irrelevant.

The first coupon payment is received at time 1 and is reinvested at 7% for one period, then at 10% for one period. The future value at time 3 of the first coupon payment is $80 \times (1.07) \times (1.10) = \$94.16$.

The second coupon payment is received at time 2 and is reinvested at 10% for one period. The future value at time 3 of the second coupon payment is $80 \times (1.10) = \$88.00$.

At time 3, you will receive the last coupon payment plus par value, for a total of $1,080. The total value of your holdings at time 3 equals $94.16 + 88.00 + 1,080 = $1,262.16. An investment of $973 has turned into $1,262.16 by reinvesting the coupon payments at the prevailing interest rates at the time the payments are received. The timeline looks like this:

The realized compound return is the rate that satisfies the equation

$$\$973 \times (1+r)^3 = \$1,262.16$$

You can solve this equation algebraically or use a financial calculator to find that the realized compound return is 9.06%.

Calculator entries: N = 3, PV = –973, PMT = 0, FV = 1262.16, Compute I/Y $\Rightarrow$ 9.06

16. The bond's value may be found with the following calculator entries. Since the bond pays interest semiannually we need to multiply N by 2 and divide the coupon rate and the discount rate by 2.

N = 8, I/Y = 4, PMT = 27, FV = 1000, CPT PV $\Rightarrow$ 952.81
N = 6, I/Y = 4, PMT = 27, FV = 1000, CPT PV $\Rightarrow$ 963.92
N = 4, I/Y = 4, PMT = 27, FV = 1000, CPT PV $\Rightarrow$ 975.48
N = 2, I/Y = 4, PMT = 27, FV = 1000, CPT PV $\Rightarrow$ 987.50
N = 0 , I/Y = 4, PMT = 27, FV = 1000, CPT PV $\Rightarrow$ 1000.00

Years Remaining until Maturity	Bond Value	Change in Price
4 (today)	$952.81	
3	$963.92	$11.11
2	$975.48	$11.56
1	$987.50	$12.02
0 (maturity)	$1,000.00	$12.50

Since the bond is selling at a discount today its price will rise to move toward par value at maturity. The change in the price will increase as the years pass.

17. Preferred stock is sometimes called a "hybrid" security because it has some features that are similar to common stock and some that are similar to debt.

   In the event of bankruptcy, obligations to preferred stockholders come after obligations to bondholders but before obligations to common stockholders.

   Like bondholders, preferred stockholders do not typically have voting rights. Unlike bondholders, they may receive the right to vote in unusual circumstances, such as when dividends have been skipped several times in a row.

   The dividends on preferred stock are usually stated as a percentage of par value or as a fixed dollar amount, although there are some issues that have adjustable rates. In this way, preferred stock is similar to bonds, which are also fixed-income investments. Dividends may also be cumulative, meaning that if they are skipped the corporation owes them to the preferred stockholders and will make payment when the cash flow situation improves.

   Like common stock dividends, if a preferred dividend is skipped it won't drive the firm into bankruptcy. Also, preferred dividends paid by the firm are not tax deductible. This is in contrast to the interest paid on bonds, which is tax deductible.

   For tax purposes, a 70% dividend exclusion applies to preferred stock dividends received by firms. That is, only 30% of the amount received is taxable. This differs from the treatment of interest income received from bonds held by firms, which is 100% taxable.

18. CDOs are collateralized debt obligations and emerged as a mechanism to reallocate credit risk in the fixed-income market. Financial institutions create CDOs by establishing a Structured Investment Vehicle (SIV), which are separate legal entities. The SIV then raises funds by issuing debt (often short-term commercial paper) and uses those funds to purchase other debt that is then pooled together and sold.

19. Mortgage-backed CDOs were an investment disaster in 2007. The problem occurred because CDOs were formed from sub-prime variable rate loans. The individuals taking out these loans did not qualify for conventional mortgages; thus, they had no place to turn if they needed to refinance. Taking out a variable rate loan when interest rates are very low is always a concern because as interest rates rise, payments will rise when the interest rate resets. Unsurprisingly, interest rates rose, as did the rates on the sub-prime mortgage pool. However, the homeowners were already stretched financially and many were not able to meet the new payment. Moreover, they did not have the credit standing to permit them to refinance. Moreover, this combined with a stalling housing market where prices were flat or falling. Thus, these homeowners could not sell their home. This resulted in many loans defaulting, which hurt the homeowners, and investors in these CDOs.

Chapter 15 Answers
The Term Structure of Interest Rates

1. The price of a 2-year zero-coupon bond is the face value discounted by the relevant required rate of return (yield to maturity), or $\$1,000 / (1.05)^2 = \$907.03$. The calculator entries would be N = 2, I/Y = 5, PMT = 0, FV = 1000, Compute PV $\Rightarrow$ 907.03.

2. The price of a 3-year zero-coupon bond is the face value discounted by the relevant required rate of return (yield to maturity), or $\$1,000 / (1.06)^3 = \$839.62$. The calculator entries would be N = 3, I/Y = 6, PMT = 0, FV = 1000, Compute PV $\Rightarrow$ 839.62.

3. The price of a 4-year zero-coupon bond is the face value discounted by the relevant required rate of return (yield to maturity), or $\$1,000 / (1.08)^4 = \$735.03$. The calculator entries would be N = 4, I/Y = 8, PMT = 0, FV = 1000, Compute PV $\Rightarrow$ 735.03.

4. To compute the price, you can consider each of the bond's cash flows as having a separate maturity date, then discount each cash flow at the corresponding required rate of return. The cash flows and the calculations are shown in the table below. The total present value of the cash flows is $\$1,074.40$, which equals the price of the bond.

Time (t)	CF_t	Calculation of $PV(CF_t)$	$PV(CF_t)$
1	\$100.00	$\$100/1.04^1 = \$95.24$	\$95.24
2	\$100.00	$\$100/1.05^2 = \$89.00$	\$89.00
3	\$100.00	$\$100/1.06^3 = \$81.63$	\$81.63
4	\$1,100.00	$\$100/1.08^4 = \$808.53$	\$808.53
		Total	**\$1,074.40**

5. The yield to maturity is the rate that equates the present value of the cash flows to the price of the bond. Using a calculator to get the answer, N = 4, PV = –1074.40, PMT = 100, FV = 1000, Compute I/Y $\Rightarrow$ 7.77. So the YTM equals 7.77%.

6. The yield to maturity on a 2-year zero-coupon bond is the y_2 that solves the equation $\$898.47 = \$1,000 / (1 + y_2)^2$. To find the answer with a calculator, use N = 2, PV = 898.47, PMT = 0, FV = 1000, Compute I/Y $\Rightarrow$ 5.50.

7. The yield to maturity on a 3-year zero-coupon bond is the y_2 that solves the equation $\$831.92 = \$1,000 / (1+y_3)^3$. To find the answer with a calculator, use N = 3, PV = 831.92, PMT = 0, FV = 1000, Compute I/Y $\Rightarrow$ 6.33.

8. The prices of the bonds and their yields must conform to the relationship

$$(1 + y_3)^3 = (1 + y_2)^2 (1 + f_3), \text{ or}$$

$$(1.0633)^3 = (1.055)^2 (1 + f_3), \text{ so}$$

$$1 + f_3 = (1.0633)^3 / (1.055)^2 = 1.08, \text{ and } f_3 = 8.0\%$$

An alternative approach to solving this problem is to realize that we are seeking the discount factor that will make the price of a 3-year bond equal to that of a 2-year bond if it is discounted for an additional period. Therefore, we can find the percentage difference between the prices and that will give us the forward rate: (898.47 / 831.92) – 1 = 8%.

9. First, we need to calculate the YTMs for the 1-year and the 4-year zero-coupon bonds (since we already calculated the 2-year and 3-year YTMs above.
   The value of y_1, using the calculator, is N = 1, PV = 952.38, PMT = 0, FV = 1000, Compute I/Y $\Rightarrow$ 5.00.
   The value of y_4, using the calculator, is N = 4, PV = 763.23, PMT = 0, FV = 1000, Compute I/Y $\Rightarrow$ 6.99.
   So the relevant yields to maturity are y_1 = 5.00%, y_2 = 5.50%, y_3 = 6.33%, and y_4 = 6.99%.
   Then we can consider each of the bond's payments as having its own maturity date and calculate the price using the associated interest rate. This yields a price of $1,176.75. The calculations are shown in the table below.

Time (t)	CFt	Calculation of PV(CF$_t$)	PV(CFt)
1	$120.00	$120 / 1.05^1 = $114.29	$114.29
2	$120.00	$120 / 1.055^2 = $107.82	$107.82
3	$120.00	$120 / 1.0633^3 = $99.83	$99.83
4	$1,120.00	$1120 / 1.0699^4 = $854.82	$854.82
		Total	$1,176.75

10. The implied forward rate for each period is $f_n = \dfrac{(1+y_n)^n}{(1+y_{n-1})^{n-1}} - 1$. The calculations are shown below.

time	YTM (y_n)	f_n	forward rate
1	5.00%		
2	5.50%	$f_2 = (1.055)^2 / (1.05)^1 = 6.00\%$	**6.00%**
3	6.33%	$f_3 = (1.0633)^3 / (1.055)^2 = 8.00\%$	**8.00%**
4	6.99%	$f_4 = (1.0699)^4 / (1.0633)^3 = 9.00\%$	**9.00%**

11. If the implied forward rates stay the same, but one year has passed, we have $f_1 = 6.00\%$, $f_2 = 8.00\%$, and $f_3 = 9.00\%$. We need to treat each of the bond's cash flows as having a separate maturity and discount by the rates that apply. The value of the bond would be $100/(1.06) + $100/[(1.08)(1.06)] + $1,100/[(1.09)(1.08)(1.09) = $1,063.22.

12. The forward rate for year 3 is one plus the yield to maturity on the 3-year bond raised to the 3rd power [$(1 + y_3)^3$], divided by the product of one plus each period's required return $(1 + f_1)(1 + f_2)$, minus one. The formula is $f_3 = \dfrac{(1+y_3)^3}{(1+f_1)(1+f_2)} - 1$.

So $f_3 = (1.068)^3 / [(1.059)(1.066)] - 1 = 7.91\%$.

13. a. The forward rate of interest for the second year is the value of f_2 that satisfies the equation $(1.079)^2 = (1.630) \times (1 + f_2)$. Solving for f_2: $(1 + f_2) = (1.079)^2 / (1.630) = 1.0952408$, so $f_2 \approx 9.52\%$

b. According to the expectations hypothesis the expected value of the one-year interest rate for next year equals the forward rate of 9.52%.

c. According to the liquidity preference theory, the forward rate equals the expected rate in the next period plus a positive premium to induce investors to hold longer-term bonds. The relationship is $f_2 = E(r_2) + $ Liquidity Premium. Since the liquidity premium is a positive number, the expected short-term interest rate next year must be less than 9.52%.

14. The pure yield curve is a plot of yield to maturity vs. time to maturity, using the yields for zero-coupon Treasuries. The graph is shown below.
Since the yield curve is upward sloping through the 5th year, investors expect that short-term rates will be higher during that period than they are today. That is, they expect that the 3-month rate will be above 3.70% when 5 years have passed. Between 5 and 10 years from now, the expectation is that short-term rates will fall. In this segment, the yield curve has a negative slope.

Then short-term rates are expected to rise again (between the 10th year and the 15th year), as reflected in the upward slope of the curve.

However, the expectation is that after 15 years short-term rates will begin to fall again. The downward slope in the yield curve is a sign of this expectation. That is, the 3-month rate that prevails 20 years from now is expected to be lower than the 3-month rate that prevails 15 years from now.

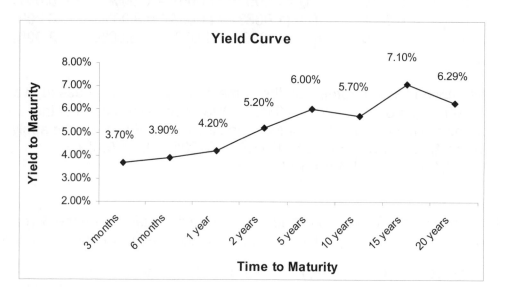

15. Both yield curves plot yield to maturity vs. time to maturity. A pure yield curve is based on the zero-coupon component of stripped Treasuries. An on-the-run yield curve uses recently issued coupon bonds that are selling at or near par value. The coupon bonds have greater liquidity, so the on-the-run yield curve is the one typically seen in the financial press.

16. Treasury STRIPS are created by stripping coupon and par value payments from Treasury bonds to create STRIPS. STRIPS are essentially zero coupon bonds and stripping is the process of creating these securities. Bond reconstitution is the process of purchasing STRIPS and putting them back together to recreate a whole Treasury bond. Arbitrage is an action taken to earn economic profit when the Law of One Price does not hold. The Law of One Price says that two identical goods must sell for the same price. Thus, a basic extension to this principle would suggest that a Treasury bond should be worth the sum of its parts (alternatively speaking the sum of the discounted cash flows) and that a Treasury bond and the STRIPS that could be used to reconstitute the bond should have equal value. If they do not, the Law of One Price has been violated and arbitrage should occur in efficient markets.

17 If the price of a Treasury bond was more than the price of the STRIPS required to reconstitute the bond, the Law of One Price has been violated and you can make an arbitrage profit. To make a profit, you should purchase the STRIPS, reconstitute the bond, and sell the bond for a price higher than the price that you paid for the STRIPS. Once you begin buying the STRIPS the increased demand will cause their price to rise (you will probably not be the lone bidder as other will have also seen this opportunity). Moreover, as you begin to sell the reconstituted bonds, the supply of bonds will increase causing their price to fall (again, you will not be alone in selling reconstituted bonds). Thus, the act of arbitrage will cause the prices of the reconstituted Treasury bonds and the equivalent STRIPS to change until the Law of One Price holds and the arbitrage opportunity is eliminated. Note: This example ignores all transactions costs that can permit small deviations from parity to exist within a narrow band.

Chapter 16 Answers
Managing Bond Portfolios

1. Duration is a simple summary statistic that provides the effective average maturity of the portfolio based on the present values of a bond's cash flows. Duration is important because it may be used to immunize the portfolio from interest rate risk. Additionally, duration is an indication of the interest rate sensitivity of the portfolio.

2. Convexity is important because duration is only an approximation of the change in the price of a bond for a small change in yield. Duration always understates the value of a bond; it underestimates the increase in bond prices when interest rates decrease and overestimates the decline in bond prices when interest rates increase. Therefore, convexity allows us to improve on the duration approximation for bond price changes.

3. The calculation of duration is shown below. An 8% discount rate is used because the bond is selling at par; therefore, the required rate of return must equal the coupon rate. To calculate each weight, divide the PV of each CF by the sum of the CFs (the price of the bond).

Year	CF	PV of CF@8%	Weight * Yr.
1	$80	$74.07	(0.07407) (1) = 0.07407
2	$80	$68.59	(0.06859) (2) = 0.13718
3	$80	$63.51	(0.06351) (3) = 0.19053
4	$80	$58.80	(0.02880) (4) = 0.23520
5	$1080	$735.03	(0.73503) (5) = 3.67515
	Sum	**$1000.00**	**4.31213 years (duration)**

Modified duration = 4.31213 years/1.08 = 3.99 years.

4. The percent change in price ($\Delta P/P$) equals $(-D^*) (\Delta y)$ or $(-8.32) (0.01) = -8.32\%$. Given a $1000 par value bond this would be $-\$83.20$.

5. No calculation is required to answer this problem. Ceteris paribus, duration is positively related to time to maturity and negatively related to coupon rate. Therefore, the 15-year bonds would have longer durations than the 5-year bonds. Considering the different coupons on the 15-year bonds leads to the conclusion that the zero-coupon bond would have a longer duration than the 8% coupon bond. So in this case the 15-year zero-coupon bond has the longest duration.

6. The bond prices and calculations are shown below.

Par	$1,000	$1,000	$1,000
Coupon Rate	6%	6%	6%
Years to Maturity	12	12	12
Yield	5.90%	**6.40%**	6.90%
Price	$1,008.43	$967.19	$928.13
% Change in Price	4.26%	--	–4.04%

N = 12, I/Y = 5.9, PMT = 60, FV = 1,000, CPT PV $\Rightarrow$ 1,008.43
N = 12, I/Y = 6.4, PMT = 60, FV = 1,000, CPT PV $\Rightarrow$ 967.19
N = 12, I/Y = 6.9, PMT = 60, FV = 1,000, CPT PV $\Rightarrow$ 928.13

This confirms that bond prices and yields are inversely related.

The percentage changes in price relative to the starting point of $967.19 are $1,008.43/$967.19 – 1 = 4.26%, and $928.13/$967.19 – 1 = –4.04%.
This shows that a decrease in a bond's yield to maturity will result in a larger price change than an equal increase in its yield to maturity. This is convexity, which is appealing to bond investors.

7. The duration of a perpetuity is $(1 + y) / y$. Thus, the duration of a perpetuity is determined by the yield and is independent of the cash flow. The duration would be $(1.09 / .09) = 12.11$ years.

8. Modified duration, D^*, equals the Macaulay duration divided by $(1 + y)$ or $D^* = D / (1 + y)$. In this case $D^* = 12.45 / (1.1) = 11.32$. [Note: For bonds that pay interest semi-annually, we use $y/2$, the semi-annual rate, in the equation.]

9. A basis point equals .01%, or .0001. If the duration is 5.25, the modified duration, D^*, is $D / (1 + y) = 5.25 / 1.085 = 4.84$. Therefore the percentage change in price will be $\Delta P/P = (–D^*) (\Delta y) = (–4.84) (–0.0031) = 1.50\%$. Since y is decreasing by .31%, P will increase by 1.50%.

10. The duration-with-convexity rule says that the percentage change in the price would be $\Delta P/P = (–D^*) (\Delta y) + (1/2) (Convexity) (\Delta y)^2$. Therefore, the percentage price change would be $(–14.2) (–.01) + (1/2) (185) (–.01)^2 = .142 + .00925 = .15125$, or approximately 15.1%.

11. The two types of risk fixed-income investors face are price risk and reinvestment rate risk. Interest rate changes have opposite effects on the types of risk. If interest rates increase, bond prices will decline and the investor will suffer a capital loss. However, the coupon interest received can be reinvested at the higher interest rate and will grow to a higher future value. The opposite effects occur when interest rates decline – bond prices rise, but coupon interest is reinvested at a lower rate. If an investor chooses a bond with a duration equal to the duration of his liabilities, the two effects will offset each other and the liabilities will be covered at the end of the investment horizon.

12. a. The calculations for the duration of the liability are shown in the table below.

time (t)	CF_t	$PV(CF_t)$	Weight = $PV(CF_t)$/Total PV	t × PV(CFt)
3	$60,000.00	$48,977.87	0.30696	0.9209
8	$190,000.00	$110,581.73	0.69304	5.5443
	Total PV	$159,559.60	**Duration =**	**6.4652**

Calculator entries:
N = 3, I/Y = 7, PMT = 0, FV = 60,000, CPT PV ⇒ 48,977.87
N = 8, I/Y = 7, PMT = 0, FV = 190,000, CPT PV ⇒ 110,581.73

   b. The duration of the zero-coupon bond equals its maturity, 2 years. The duration of the perpetuity equals $(1 + y)/y = 1.07/.07 = 15.29$ years.
   c. Choose the proportions that will make the duration of your asset holdings equal to the duration of the liability:

   $w \times 2 + (1–w) \times 15.29 = 6.4652$
   $2w + 15.29 – 15.29w = 6.4652$
   $–13.29w = –8.8248$
   $w = .6639$
   $1 – w = .3361$

   So put 66.39% in the zero-coupon bond and 33.61% in the perpetuity.

   d. To fully fund the liability, apply the weights to the total present value of the liability:
   Amount in the zero-coupon bond = $.6639 \times \$159,559.60 = \$105,932.96$
   Amount in the perpetuity = $.3361 \times \$159,559.60 = \$53.626.64$

   e. The face value of your investment in the zero-coupon bond is the amount to which it will mature in 2 years: $\$105,932.96 \times (1.07)^2 = \$121,282.65$

13. Cash flow matching is implemented by purchasing an asset that has the same duration as the liability and has a future payout amount that exactly equals the amount needed to meet the liability. For example, suppose you are obligated to pay $45,000 in three years and that there is a zero-coupon bond available with a 3-year maturity that is selling at a yield of 5.0%. You would purchase zero-coupon bonds that will mature to $45,000 in three years. The bonds would have a present value equal to $45,000/$1.05^3$ = $38,872.69. The portfolio would be immunized and no rebalancing would be necessary.

A dedication strategy is similar to a cash flow matching strategy but it involves more than one period. Assets are selected to provide the exact amount of cash flows needed at exactly the time that each liability must be paid. This leads to immunization without a need for rebalancing.

14. a. There are 4 years remaining until the terminal value must be reached. At an interest rate of 8%, the present value needed to grow into the required $21 million is $21,000,000 / 1.08^4 = $15,435,626.91. If the portfolio's value is $16 million you don't need to immunize because this is more than enough to reach the target value at the current interest rate.
    b. There are 3 years remaining, so the present value needed is $21,000,000 / 1.073^3 = $16,998,872.98. If the portfolio is worth only $16 million you will need to immunize to ensure that the terminal value of $21 million is reached. At the current interest rate, the $16 million would only grow to $16,000,000 × 1.073^3 = $19,766,016.27.
    c. With 2 years left and an interest rate of 8.7%, the trigger point is $21,000,000 / 1.087^2 = $17,772,978.13. If the portfolio's value is $17.8 million you will not need to immunize.
    d. There is 1 year left so the trigger point is $21,000,000 / 1.094 = $19,195,612.43. If the portfolio's value is $19 million you will need to immunize to ensure that the terminal value equals $21 million.

15. a. pure yield pickup swap
    b. tax swap
    c. substitution swap
    d. intermarket spread swap
    e. pure yield pickup swap

16. The six general properties regarding the interest rate sensitivity of bond prices are:
    1. Bond prices and yields are inversely related: as yields increase, bond prices fall; as yields fall, bond prices rise.
    2. An increase in a bond's required yield to maturity results in smaller price changes than a decrease of equal magnitude.
    3. Prices of long-term bonds are more sensitive to interest rate changes than prices of short-term bonds.
    4. The sensitivity of bond prices to changes in yields increases at a decreasing rate as maturity increases. Interest rate risk is less than proportional to bond maturity.
    5. Interest rate risk is inversely related to the bond's coupon rate. Prices of low coupon bonds are more sensitive to changes in interest rates than prices of high coupon bonds.
    6. The sensitivity of a bond's price to a change in its required yield is inversely related to the yield to maturity at which the bond is currently selling.

17. The five rules of duration are:
    1. The duration of a zero-coupon bond equals its time to maturity.
    2. Holding maturity constant, a bond's duration is inversely related to its coupon rate (the duration is lower when the coupon rate is higher).
    3. Holding the coupon rate constant, a bond's duration generally increases with its time to maturity. Duration always increases for bonds trading at par or at a premium to par.
    4. Holding other factors constant, the duration of a coupon bond is higher when the bond's yield to maturity is lower.
    5. The duration of a level perpetuity is:
       $$\text{Duration of perpetuity} = (1 + y)/y.$$

Chapter 17 Answers
Macroeconomic and Industry Analysis

1. a. Gross Domestic Product is a measure of the economy's total production of goods and services. It is used to evaluate the level of a country's economic growth.
   b. The Unemployment Rate is the percentage of the labor force that is actively seeking employment but not yet working. It is used to assess how close the economy is to operating at full capacity.
   c. Inflation is the rate at which the general level of prices is rising. The inflation rate is considered in conjunction with the productivity of the economy to determine whether the economy is "overheated."

2. "Crowding out" is a phenomenon that occurs when the government borrows large amounts of money, usually to cover budgetary shortfalls due to deficit spending. The demand for money is so strong that it forces interest rates to rise to a point where businesses cannot afford to borrow. This leads to a decline in business investment.

3. Start by calculating revenue, which is the price times the quantity sold. Then subtract fixed cost from revenue. Next subtract variable cost, which is calculated as variable cost per unit times the number of units sold. Finally, multiply the result by one minus the marginal tax rate.

Firm A if Economy is in Recession

Revenue	$	1,176,000	p * Q
Fixed Cost		450,000	given
Variable Cost		470,400	v * Q
Taxable Income	$	255,600	Revenue – Fixed Cost – Variable Cost
Tax		76,680	.3 * Taxable Income
After-tax Profit	$	178,920	Taxable Income – Tax

4. The calculations are similar to those in problem 3 and are shown below.

Firm B if Economy is in Recession

Revenue	$	1,176,000	p * Q
Fixed Cost		260,000	given
Variable Cost		705,600	v * Q
Taxable Income	$	210,400	Revenue – Fixed Cost – Variable Cost
Tax		63,120	.3 * Taxable Income
After-tax Profit	$	147,280	Taxable Income – Tax

5. The calculations are similar to those in problem 3 and are shown below.

Firm A if Economy is Strong

Revenue	$	1,800,000	p * Q
Fixed Cost		450,000	given
Variable Cost		720,000	v * Q
Taxable Income	$	630,000	Revenue – Fixed Cost – Variable Cost
Tax		189,000	.3 * Taxable Income
After-tax Profit	$	441,000	Taxable Income – Tax

6. The calculations are similar to those in problem 3 and are shown below.

Firm B if Economy is Strong

Revenue	$	1,800,000	p * Q
Fixed Cost		260,000	given
Variable Cost		1,080,000	v * Q
Taxable Income	$	460,000	Revenue – Fixed Cost – Variable Cost
Tax		138,000	.3 * Taxable Income
After-tax Profit	$	322,000	Taxable Income – Tax

7. The degree of operating leverage is the percent change in after tax profit divided by the percent change in sales, or

% Δ in profit = (441,000 – 178,920) / 178,920 = 1.46479 (146.48%)
% Δ in sales = (1,800,000 – 1,176,000) / 1,176,000 = 0.53061 (53.06%)
DOL = (1.46479 / 0.53061) = 2.76

8. The degree of operating leverage is the percent change in after tax profit divided by the percent change in sales, or

% Δ in profit = (322,000 – 147,280) / 147,280 = 1.18631
% Δ in sales = (1,800,000 – 1,176,000) / 1,176,000 = 0.53061 (53.06%)
DOL = (1.18631 / 0.53061) = 2.24

9. a. A peak is the transition from the end of an economic expansion to the start of an economic contraction.
    b. A trough is the transition from an economic recession to an economic recovery.
    c. A cyclical industry is one that has above average sensitivity to the state of the economy. Cyclical industries are those whose performance moves in tandem with the economy, doing well when the economy is strong and declining when the economy is weak. Examples include durable consumer goods such as automobiles and refrigerators, and capital goods that are needed by businesses.

d. A defensive industry is relatively insensitive to the state of the economy. The performance of defensive industries remains relatively stable whether the economy is strong or weak. Examples include food, pharmaceuticals, tobacco, and utilities. These are things people will purchase regardless of market conditions.

10. Leading economic indicators are economic data series that tend to rise or fall before the general level of economic activity. If the economy has been in recession and the leading economic indicators are rising, it may be a signal that a turnaround is imminent. There are 10 leading economic indicators.
Lagging economic indicators are economic data series that follow the changes in the general level of economic activity. There are 7 lagging economic indicators.
Coincident economic indicators are economic data series that tend to change around the same time as the general level of economic activity. There are 4 coincident economic indicators.
a. industrial production – coincident
b. money supply (M2) – leading
c. new orders for nondefense capital goods – leading
d. change in the consumer price index for services – lagging
e. initial claims for unemployment insurance – leading
f. average duration of unemployment – lagging
g. manufacturing and trade sales – coincident
h. new private housing units authorized by local building permits – leading
i. ratio of consumer installment credit outstanding to personal income – lagging

11. The three factors that determine the sensitivity of a firm's earnings to the business cycle are the sensitivity of sales, the firm's operating leverage, and the firm's financial leverage.

The degree to which sales change as the economy changes will depend on whether the items sold are necessities or luxuries, and on how much of an individual's budget is typically spent on the items. Food, drugs, and medical services, for example, are relatively insensitive to changes in the business cycle because they are necessities.

Operating leverage reflects the degree to which a firm's costs are fixed or variable. Firms with high fixed costs cannot adjust as readily to reduced demand for their goods or services. They are more likely to have difficulties during economic downturns.

Financial leverage provides a measure of how much the firm uses borrowing to finance its operations. If a firm borrows substantially to support its operations it will have fixed interest liabilities that must be paid regardless of the level of sales. When there is an economic downturn this type of firm is especially prone to financial difficulties.

12. The four stages in the industry life cycle are:
    a. Start-up stage – This stage is characterized by a new technology or product. In this stage, it is difficult to predict which firms will become industry leaders. Industry sales will grow rapidly.
    b. Consolidation stage – After the product becomes established, industry leaders emerge. The performance of surviving firms will more closely track the overall industry. Industry growth will be more rapid than the overall economy.
    c. Maturity stage – The product has reached full potential and has become relatively standardized. Competition is now based largely on price and profit margins narrow. Industry growth will become close to that of the overall economy.
    d. Relative decline stage – The industry might grow at a rate less than the economy overall or may even shrink. This is often due to obsolescence of the product.

13. Porter's five determinants of competition are:
    a. Threat of entry – High barriers to entry make it difficult for new firms to enter and compete in the industry. If barriers to entry are low, new entrants will put pressure on prices and profits.
    b. Rivalry between existing competitors – This refers to the nature of competition between firms in the industry. If few firms exist, competition may be more friendly and based on differentiation. However, as the number of firms increase, competition may turn toward price.
    c. Pressure from substitute products – The interest here is how products from a related but different industry affect a given industry.
    d. Bargaining power of buyers – The issue is the structure of buyers. If only a few large buyers exist, the buyers can demand price concessions. This puts pressure on margins.
    e. Bargaining power of suppliers – If a supplier has a monopoly over a key input to an industry, the supplier could demand premium prices. This could squeeze the profits out of an industry.

14. The two broad classes of macroeconomic tools that the government can use are fiscal policy and monetary policy.

    Fiscal policy refers to government spending and taxation. Changes in fiscal policy have a quick impact on the economy but the formulation and implementation of policy is very slow.

    Monetary policy refers to the manipulation of the money supply. The Fed does this through open market operations and changes in reserve requirements and the discount rate.

15. Sector rotation is tilting the portfolio more heavily toward industry or sector groups that are expected to perform well and away from sectors that are expected to do poorly. In developing a sector rotation plan, many factors must be considered. Both global and domestic economic conditions are important since economic conditions and changes in them affect demand. Changes in conditions also have a differential impact on defensive and cyclical industries. Finally, the stage of the industry's life cycle and Porter's five factors of competition need to be considered since both influence profitability.

16. A firm that is headquartered in Oklahoma cannot ignore the global economy. The firm may make sales to other countries, employ people that reside in other countries, and invest in other countries. Therefore, the firm may face price competition from similar foreign firms in both domestic and foreign markets. The firm may also face wages that are different from those paid by the foreign competition. Moreover, management may have less power to do what it wants due to the economic force of labor unions. Imports of raw material and exports of its products will be influenced by the strength of the global economy and foreign exchange rates. Interest rates in other countries may also determine part of the return on the firm's investments. Exchange rates pose an additional risk if the company wants to repatriate any foreign earnings. Countries' political and economic policies should be also be considered.

17. Demand shocks are events that affect the demand of goods and services in the economy. Positive demand shocks increase the demand for goods and services whereas negative demand shocks decrease the demand for goods and services. A few examples of positive shocks are reductions in tax rates, increases in the money supply, increases in government spending, and increases in foreign export demand. Negative demand shocks would include increases in tax rates, decreases in the money supply, decreases in government spending, and decreases in foreign export demand. Supply shocks are events that influence production capacity and costs. Examples of negative supply shocks are increases in the price of imported oil, freezes, floods, droughts that destroy large quantities of crops, or mandated increases in wages of benefits. Positive shocks would reduce costs.

Chapter 18 Answers
Equity Valuation Models

1. a. Book value is the net worth of the company as it is shown on the Balance Sheet. For a company that has $10 million in assets and $6 million in liabilities, the net worth is the difference, or $4 million. If the firm has one million shares outstanding, the book value per share is $4.
    b. Liquidation value is the amount that would be received if the assets of the firm were sold and the firm's debts were paid off. The liquidation value would be distributed to shareholders. If the market value of a firm drops below its liquidation value, the firm could become a takeover target.
    c. Replacement cost is the amount that would have to be paid to repurchase the firm's assets, minus its liabilities.
    d. Tobin's q is the ratio of a firm's market price to its replacement cost. In the long run, this ratio should equal approximately one.

2. The growth rate, g, is the product of the plowback ratio (1 – dividend payout ratio) and ROE. Denoting the plowback ratio as b, the relationship is g = ROE(b). Therefore, g = 11% (0.75) = 8.25%.

3. The value of a perpetuity is the dividend divided by the required rate of return, or $V_0 = D / k$. Therefore, $V_0 = \$4.16 / .10 = \$41.60$. Note that there is no need to use a subscript on D since dividends remain constant, and that the general denominator (k – g) reduces to k because g = 0.

4. The value of the stock is the present value of its expected cash flows. Since both amounts are expected to be received in one year, add them together and discount them by the required rate of return for one period. The result is $V_0 = (D_1 + P_1) / (1 + k) = (\$1.41 + 33)/(1.11)^1 = \$31.00$.

5. According to the CAPM, the required rate of return on any security is given by $E(R_i) = R_f + \beta_i (R_M - R_f)$. Therefore, the required return on Monarch would be $E(R_i) = 4.25\% + 1.35 (12.5\% - 4.25\%) = 15.39\%$.

6. The stock's intrinsic value is the present value of its expected cash flows. We expect to get a dividend of $2.25 and a price of $23 in one year. Thus the intrinsic value is $V_0 = (D1 + P_1) / (1+k)^1 = (\$2.25 + 23) / (1.1539)^1 = \$21.88$.

7. Given that k = 15.39% (from above) and the knowledge that the Gordon Growth Model can be stated as $P_0 = D_1 / (k-g)$, we can solve the equation for g to find that $g = k - (D_1/P_0) = .1539 - (\$2.25/\$21) = .0467$, or 4.67%.

8. According to the CAPM, the return would need to be $E(R_i) = R_f + \beta_i [E(R_m) - R_f]$, or $E(R_i) = 5\% + 1.5 (12\% - 5\%) = 15.50\%$. If beta doubled to 3.0, the return on the stock would change to $(R_i) = 5\% + 3.0 (12\% - 5\%) = 26.00\%$, which is less than double the previous return. The relationship between beta and required return is not linear.

9. The growth rate is the product of the plowback ratio and the ROE. Inserting the values we have into the equation $g = ROE (b)$ gives us $g = (.13) (.65) = 8.45\%$. The dividend should grow at a rate of 8.45%, so $D_1 = D_0 (1+g) = \$2 (1.0845) = \$2.169$.

10. a. The dividend discount model says that intrinsic value equals $D_1/(k - g)$. This implies that
    - Intrinsic value increases as the dividend per share increases.
    - Intrinsic value decreases as the market capitalization rate increases.
    - Intrinsic value increases as the expected growth rate of dividends increases.
    b. The constant growth model implies that the growth rate of the stock price will be equal to the growth rate of the dividends.

11. The intrinsic value should be the P/E times the expected EPS or 22 ($2.00) = $44.00.

12. Expected EPS would be the stock price times the reciprocal of the P/E ratio or $20(1/32) = $0.625.

13. Since growth is constant after year 3, the constant growth model can be used to find the value of the stock at year 3 (P_3) from the relationship $P_3 = D_4/(k - g)$. Then we can find the value of the stock as the sum of the discounted dividends and the discounted P_3.

$D_4 = D_3(1+g) = \$2.54(1.08) = \$2.7432$. So $P_3 = \$2.7432/(.11-.08) = \$91.44$. The relevant cash flows and their present values are shown in the table below. The value of the stock today is $71.80.

Time	Cash Flow	PV of CF @ 11%
1	$1.65	$1.65/(1.11)^1 = $1.4865
2	$1.97	$1.97/(1.11)^2 = $1.5989
3	$2.54 + 91.44 = $93.98	$93.98/(1.11)^3 = $68.7174
	Sum = V_0	**$71.8027**

14. Since growth is constant after year 3, the constant growth model can be used to find the value of the stock at year 3 (P_3) from the relationship $P_3 = D_4/(k - g)$. Then we can find the value of the stock as the sum of the discounted dividends and the discounted P_3.

$D_4 = D_3(1+g) = \$0.85(0.98) = \$0.8330$. So $P_3 = \$0.8330/(.08+.02) = \$8.33$. The relevant cash flows and their present values are shown in the table below. The value of the stock today is $8.98.

Note that the negative growth rate leads to a stock value that is lower than it would have been with a zero or a positive growth rate.

Time	Cash Flow	PV of CF @ 8%
1	$1.00	$1.00/(1.08)^1 = $0.9259
2	$0.90	$0.90/(1.08)^2 = $0.7716
3	$0.85 + $8.33 = $9.18	$9.18/(1.08)^3 = $7.2874
	Sum = V_0	**$8.9849**

15. The present value of growth opportunities plays a major role in determining current stock values. Because of anticipated future growth, some firms with low or even negative earnings may have high stock prices. Firms like amazon.com, eBay, and Google have experienced this phenomenon. These firms have been relatively successful in their enterprises since the growth has materialized to a reasonable degree. Some other firms have failed to grow and not met expectations. Growth expectations are far from certain and are continuously being revised by market participants. As expectations change, the stock prices change to reflect them.

16. Some alternative ratios are the price-to-book ratio, the price-to-cash flow ratio, and the price-to-sales ratio.

    The price-to-book ratio relates the book value per share to the price per share. Book value is based on historical costs.

    The price-to-cash flow ratio uses cash flow instead of earnings. Using cash flow eliminates the problem of lack of comparability due to accounting choices. The cash flow number used to compute this ratio can be operating cash flow or free cash flow (operating cash flow net of new investment).

    The price to sales ratio uses the stock price relative to the level of annual sales per share. It is often used for new firms that have negative accounting earnings. As the firms mature, earnings should swing to the positive side and the P/E ratio will become meaningful.

17. The free cash flow approach is an alternative to the DDM. The FCF approach can be used by a firm's management for making capital budgeting decisions, valuing acquisition targets, or valuing divisions. FCF can also be used by investors to value the firm or its stock. Two variants of the FCF approach exist. The first model is the free cash flow to equity model (FCFE) and it is very similar to the DDM. The easiest way to think about this model is that shareholders are residual claimants and therefore entitled to their proportionate share of the firm's earnings. If the firm does not pay dividends, per-share FCFE is available to the shareholder. Per share FCFE can be used with no-growth, constant growth (Gordon model), or non-constant growth DDM type models in place of the dividend. FCFF (free cash flow to the firm) is somewhat different. To use the FCFF model first the value of the firm as a whole is estimated. Then the market value of nonequity claims is subtracted, and the result is the value of the firm's equity.

18. Bushhog's FCFF can be calculated as:

    FCFF = EBIT(1 – T) + depreciation – capital expenditures – increase in NWC

    or

    800,000(.7) + 52,000 – 86,000 – 16,000 = 510,000.

Chapter 19 Answers
Financial Statement Analysis

1. The current ratio is calculated as current assets divided by current liabilities, or ($1,571,000 / $837,000) = 1.88.

2. The quick ratio is calculated as (cash plus accounts receivable) divided by current liabilities, or ($1,571,000 – $931,000)/$837,000 = 0.76.

3. The leverage ratio is calculated as assets divided by equity, or $3,090,000 / $1,378,000 = 2.24.

4. The times interest earned ratio is calculated as EBIT (Earnings Before Interest and Taxes), which is the same thing as Operating Income) divided by interest expense, or $985,000 / $60,000 = 16.42.

5. The average collection period is calculated as (average accounts receivable / sales) time 365, or {[($557,000 + $450,000)/2] / $5,600,000} (365 days) = 32.82 days.

6. The inventory turnover ratio is calculated as COGS (the Cost of Goods Sold) divided by average inventory or $3,600,000 / [($931,000 + $700,000) / 2] = 4.41.

7. The fixed asset turnover ratio is calculated as sales divided by average net fixed assets, or $5,600,000 / [($1,519,000 + $1,200,000) / 2] = 4.12.

8. The total asset turnover ratio is calculated as sales divided by average total assets, or $5,600,000 / [($3,090,000 + $2,390,000) / 2] = 2.04.

9. The return on sales ratio is calculated as operating income (which is the same thing as EBIT) divided by sales, or $985,000 / $5,600,000 = 17.59%.

10. ROE is calculated as net income divided by average equity or $700,000 / [($1,378,000 + $690,000) / 2] = 67.70%.

11. The Statement of Cash Flows is shown below.

Heavy Hog Company
2007 Statement of Cash Flows

Cash Flows from Operations		
Net Income	$	700,000
Adjustment for Depreciation Expense		500,000
Increase in Accounts Receivable		(107,000)
Increase in Inventory		(231,000)
Increase in Accounts Payable		112,000
Increase in Notes Payable		25,000
Cash Provided by Operations	**$**	**999,000**
Cash Flows from Investments		
Increase in Gross Fixed Assets	$	(819,000)
Cash Provided by Investments		**(819,000)**
Cash Flows from Financing Activities		
Decrease in Long-Term Debt		(125,000)
Increase in Common Stock		–
Dividends Paid	$	(12,000)
Cash Provided by Financing Activities		**(137,000)**
Net Increase in Cash	**$**	**43,000**

One of the less obvious calculations is the amount of dividends paid. We can find this by realizing that dividends must equal the amount of net income that was not added to Retained Earnings. The formula is Dividends Paid = Net Income – Addition to Retained Earnings. In this case, the numbers are $700,000 – (1,178,000 – 490,000) = $12,000.

Note that increases in asset accounts are uses of cash and increases in liability and equity accounts are sources of cash. For example, inventory went up by $231,000, which means that the firm used cash to increase its inventory stores. Notes Payable went up by $25,000, which implies that the firm borrowed a net amount equal to this, so it was a source of cash.

Heavy Hogs is in a relatively healthy financial situation with regard to cash flow. It has positive cash flow from operations and has made a significant investment in long-term assets. It has also used some cash to pay off a portion of its long-term debt and to pay dividends to its stockholders.

12. Accounting earnings are those that are reported on a firm's Income Statement. They are subject to the choices management makes about valuation of assets such as inventory and how to expense certain items such as bad debts, depreciation, amortization, and goodwill.

Economic earnings consist of the actual cash flows a firm would be able to pay out indefinitely if it maintained the same productive capacity as it currently has.

13. EVA = Capital Invested × (Return on Assets – Cost of Capital). For example, A;pha Athletics' EVA = $7.43 million × (.11 – .09) = $0.15 million.
A negative EVA can be caused by either a negative return on assets or the cost of capital exceeding the return on capital.

	Capital (millions)	Return on Assets	Cost of Capital	EVA (millions)
Alpha Athletics	$7.43	11.00%	9.00%	$0.15
Beta Body Builders	$19.25	–3.00%	16.00%	–$3.66
Lambda Levitators	$6.47	26.00%	18.00%	$0.52
Theta Theoretics	$2.23	24.00%	14.00%	$0.22

14. Accounting depreciation reflects the allocation of the cost of an asset over several periods rather than just during the period in which the asset was purchased. The asset is capitalized, or put on the books at its value, when it is purchased, but the cost of it is determined by allowable formulas and charged as expense gradually over several years. Firms may choose from several alternative formulas, including straight-line depreciation and accelerated depreciation methods. Accounting depreciation bears no relationship to the actual rate of use of the asset. Economic depreciation reflects the amount of a firm's operating cash flow that must be reinvested to sustain the real cash flow at its current level. It reflects the actual rate of use of the asset.

During periods of inflation, accounting depreciation will understate the true replacement cost of the asset and real economic income will be overstated. This is because accounting depreciation will be based on historical cost, while the replacement cost of the asset will be increasing.

15. Some of the factors that affect earnings quality are
   - allowance for bad debt – If the firm sets this at an impractical level to reduce bad debts expense, it would reduce the quality of earnings.
   - treatment of non-recurring items – If a firm treats charges as non-recurring to separate them from regular operating income, when in fact they are likely to happen repeatedly, it would reduce the quality of earnings.

- reserves management – A firm can set aside extra reserves during strong periods so it will be able to release the reserves in troubled times. This practice would reduce the quality of earnings.
- treatment of stock options – When calculating labor expense, FASB now requires firms to include the value of stock options given to employees as an expense. However, the value of the options may be calculated in various ways and this can affect earnings quality.
- revenue recognition – Firms generally recognize income when sales are made rather than when the actual revenue from the sale is collected (accrual accounting). If revenue collection is anticipated to be in the distant future or there is a significant probability that the revenue will not be collected, the quality of earnings is lower than it would be otherwise.
- off balance sheet assets and liabilities – If a firm does not disclose its contingent liabilities or uses leasing arrangements in a deceptive manner, its earnings quality will be lower.

16. The DuPont system is a method of decomposing ROE into components so that an analyst can more easily determine the major factor contributing to the firm's ROE. By highlighting this factor, management can more easily develop corrective action to increase future ROE. The DuPont system decomposes ROE into the following components:

$$ROE = \frac{\text{Net Profits}}{\text{Pretax Profits}} \times \frac{\text{Pretax Profits}}{\text{EBIT}} \times \frac{\text{EBIT}}{\text{Sales}} \times \frac{\text{Sales}}{\text{Assets}} \times \frac{\text{Assets}}{\text{Equity}}$$

Tax Burden	Net Profit/Pretax Profit	0.60	For every $1.00 the firm has before it pays taxes, it has $0.60 left after it pays taxes.
Margin	EBIT/Sales	0.10	For every $1.00 the firm makes in sales, it has $0.10 left after expenses are deducted, but before it has paid taxes and interest.
Leverage	Assets/Equity	1.67	For every $1.00 the firm's owners have invested, the firm has $1.67 in assets.
Turnover	Sales/Assets	1.00	For every $1.00 the firm has in assets, it has produced $1.00 in sales.
Interest Burden	Pretax Profit/EBIT	0.68	For every $1.00 the firm has after expenses are deducted but before it pays interest and taxes, it will have $0.68 left after it pays taxes.

17. Common-size analysis entails creating common-size financial statements for comparison to the common-size financial statements of another firm, or group of firms. Common-size analysis is useful because firms of different sizes can have vastly different levels of assets, liabilities, income, and expenses which makes direct comparison difficult. By recasting financial statements into common-size, comparison with different size firms is possible. Common-size income statements are created by dividing all items on the income statement by total revenue. Common-size balance sheets are created by dividing all items on the balance sheet by total assets.

Chapter 20 Answers
Options Markets: Introduction

1. a. A call option is in the money if the strike price is less than the current stock price. A put option is in the money if the strike price is more than the current stock price. An option will be exercised if it is in the money.

    The profit from a call option that is in the money equals the current stock price minus the exercise price minus the amount of the premium paid.
    Profit on the ABC call = $10.26 – 10.00 – 1.10 = –$0.84.
    Return = –$0.84 / $1.10 = –73.36%.
    Note that being in the money doesn't guarantee a positive return. It is still better to exercise the call as long as it is in the money, however, because if it is not exercised the return will be –100%.

    The profit on a call option that is out of the money equals the negative value of the premium.
    Profit on the XYZ call = –$1.05.
    Return = –$1.05 / $1.05 = –100%.

    The profit from a put option that is in the money equals the exercise price minus the current stock price minus the amount of the premium paid.
    Profit on the XYZ put = $25.00 – 23.93 – 2.25 = –$1.18.
    Return = –$1.18 / $2.25 = –52.44%.
    Note that being in the money doesn't guarantee a positive return. It is still better to exercise the put as long as it is in the money, however, because if it is not exercised the return will be –100%.

    The profit on a put option that is out of the money equals the negative value of the premium.
    Profit on the ABC put = –$0.95.
    Return = – $0.95 / $0.95 = –100%.

Company	Option	Strike	Today's Stock Price	In/Out of the Money?	Premium	Exercise?	Profit	Return
ABC	call	10	10.26	in	1.10	yes	–$0.84	–73.36%
ABC	put	10	10.26	out	0.95	no	–$0.95	–100%
XYZ	call	25	23.93	out	1.05	no	–$1.05	–100%
XYZ	put	25	23.93	in	2.25	yes	–$1.18	–52.44%

b. Profit on ABC call = $11.23 – 10.00 – 1.10 = $0.13
Return on ABC call = $0.13 / $1.10 = 11.82%.

Profit on ABC put = – $0.95
Return on ABC call = – $0.95 / $0.95 = – 100%.

Profit on XYZ call = $27.00 – 25.00 – 1.05 = $0.95
Return on XYZ call = $0.95 / $1.05 = 90.48%.

Profit on XYZ put = –$2.25
Return on XYZ call = –$2.25 / $2.25 = –100%.

Company	Option	Strike	Today's Stock Price	In/Out of the Money?	Premium	Exercise?	Profit	Return
ABC	call	10	11.23	in	1.10	yes	$0.13	11.82%
ABC	put	10	11.23	out	0.95	no	–$0.95	–100%
XYZ	call	25	27.00	in	1.05	yes	$0.95	90.48%
XYZ	put	25	27.00	out	2.25	no	–$2.25	–100%

2. The items differ as described below.
   - terms of the contract – can be tailored to suit the traders' needs OTC, but are standardized for maturity date, strike price, and number of shares on exchanges
   - costs – relatively high for OTC options, lower for exchange-traded options
   - depth of trading – better for exchange-traded options because of standardization of the options contracts
   - ease of trading and liquidity – better for exchange-traded options because of standardization of contracts and depth of trading

3. a. The value of a call option is negatively related to its exercise price and positively related to the price of the underlying stock. The higher the exercise price, the more the call option holder must pay to purchase the stock if the option is exercised. This reduces the potential profit of the call option. The higher the price of the underlying stock, the more likely it is that the call option will be in the money, and the greater the potential for profit.
   b. The relationships for put options are opposite those of the call options. The value of a put option is positively related to its exercise price and negatively related to the price of the underlying stock. The higher the exercise price, the more the put option holder will receive when the stock is sold to the writer of the option if it is exercised. This increases the potential profit of the put option. The lower the price of the underlying stock, the more likely it is that the put option will be in the money, and the greater the potential for profit.

4. The features of the Option Clearing Corporation (OCC):
    *   ownership – The OCC is owned by the exchanges on which stock options are traded.
    *   relationship to options traders – The OCC stands between the traders, effectively buying options from traders who write them and selling options to traders who buy them. In this way the OCC guarantees that the contracts will be honored.
    *   interaction with member firms – The OCC contacts member firms as it needs them to honor exercised options contracts. If a call option on IBM stock is exercised, for example, the member firm will choose one of its clients who wrote a call option on IBM and the client will be required to buy the shares of IBM from the option exerciser at the specified strike price.
    *   margin requirements – The OCC requires options writers to post margin to ensure that they will honor their obligations. Options holders do not have to post margin because they pay the premium up front and will only exercise the option if it becomes profitable. Margin requirements are higher for options that are in the money, and also depend on whether the underlying asset is held by the writer (call options) and the value of the underlying asset.

5. The breakeven price is the exercise price minus the premium or $60 – $4 = $56. Since you have the right to sell the stock for $60, if the holder chooses to exercise the put and you buy the stock for $56 and sell it for $60, that will give you a net of $4, which exactly equals the premium you paid to write the put.

6. The breakeven price is the exercise price plus the premium or $60 + $3 = $63. If you choose to exercise the call you can buy the stock for $60. If you can sell the stock in the market for $63, you will exactly offset what you paid for the stock and the $3 premium you paid when you bought the call.

7. a. The graph below shows that for prices less than the strike price of $30 the option would expire worthless and your profit would be –$6, the premium you paid. When the price rises above $30 you will exercise the call. At a stock price of $36 ($30 + 6) you have recovered the amount of the premium and break even. Above $36, there is a net profit.

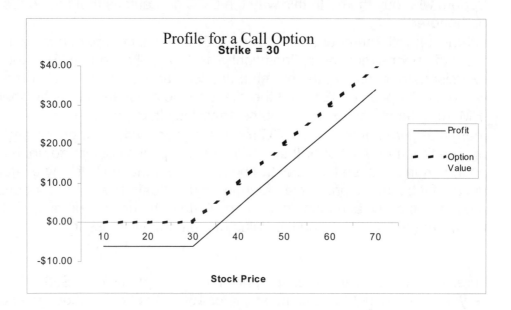

b. The perspective of the call writer is a mirror image of that of the call holder. The writer keeps the premium of $6 for stock prices below the strike price. When the stock price rises above $36, the option writer starts to lose money.

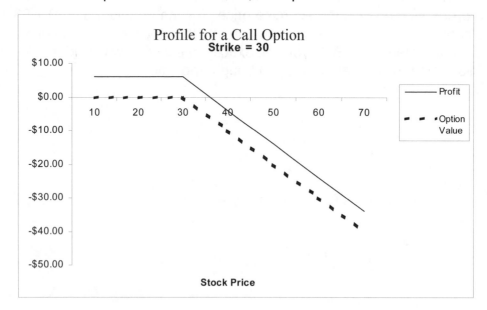

8. Your maximum profit would occur at a price of $25 or more (buy at $20 and sell at $25). Your profit would be the $5 per share difference between the exercise prices plus the difference in premiums that you paid and received (–$2 + $1 = –$1). Therefore, the net gain would be $5 – $1 = $4 per unit. Since there are 100 shares per contract, the gain would be $4 (100) = $400.

9. The profit would be:
Profit on purchased call = spot price – (strike price + premium) = $23 – ($20 + $2) = $1
Profit on written call = the premium (since the option is out-of-the-money and the holder will not choose to exercise it) = $1
Net profit = $1 + $1 = $2 per share. Since there are 100 shares per contract the profit is $200.

10. The maximum loss from writing an uncovered call is unlimited. However, since you purchased a call as well, this position is not uncovered. In fact, you profit if the stock price increases. In this case, your maximum loss would occur if both options expire worthless. The loss would be the difference between the premium that you paid ($2) and the premium that you received ($1), or –$1 per share times 100 shares = a maximum of a $100 loss.

11. The breakeven point is the strike price plus the premium that you paid minus the premium that you received or $20 + $2 – $1 = $21.
You will exercise the call you bought by paying $20 for the stock, then sell the stock in the market for $21. The $1 you make will exactly offset the net premium ($1 – 2 = –$1).

12. The maximum loss occurs when you lose both premiums or –$1 + (–$4) = –$5 (100 shares) = $500 loss.

13. You can break even by exercising either the call or the put. By buying one of each you have enacted a straddle position.

The call will be exercised for prices above $55. In this range, the put will expire worthless. When the call is exercised, the profit will be P-55-1-4. The breakeven point is when this quantity equals zero, so we need to solve the equation for P. 0 = P-55-1-4, so P = 60. (In other words, the breakeven price equals the strike price plus the premiums.)

The put will be exercised for prices below $55. In this range, the call will expire worthless. When the put is exercised, the profit will be $55-P-1-4. The breakeven point occurs when this quantity equals zero, so we need to solve the equation for P. 0 = 55-P-1-4, so P = 50. (In other words, the breakeven price equals the strike price minus the premiums.)

Thus, if price increases above $60 or decreases below $50, a profit is realized. For prices between $55 and $60, you will incur a loss on your position. If you need to convince yourself of this, build a table with varying prices and calculate the profit for each price.

14. Put-call parity says that $C + (X / (1+r_f)) = S_o + P$. Subtracting S_o from both sides and inserting known values gives $\$7 + (86/1.04) - 80 = P = \$9.69$.

15. Put-call parity says that $C + (X / (1+r_f)) = S_o + P$. Subtracting $(X / (1+r_f))$ from both sides and inserting known values gives $C = \$92 + 6 - (90/1.04) = \$11.46$.

16. The difference between American and European options is that American options can be exercised at any time (on or before) the expiration day whereas European options can only be exercised on the expiration day.

17. Explain the major characteristics of the following types of exotic options:
    a. Asian – the payoff depends on the *average* price of the underlying asset during some portion of the life of the option.
    b. Barrier – the payoff depends on not only on an asset price at expiration, but also on whether the price crossed through some barrier.
    c. Lookback – the payoff depends in part on the minimum or maximum price of the underlying asset during the life of the option.
    d. Digital – the payoff is fixed and depends on whether a specified condition occurred.
    e. Currency-translated – either the payoff or asset price is denominated in a foreign currency.

18. Explain the following option strategies:
    a. Covered call – the purchase of a stock and the sale of a call on the stock.
    b. Protective put – the purchase of a stock and a put on the stock.
    c. Straddle – the purchase (or sale) of a put and a call on a stock that have the same exercise price and expiration date.
    d. Strips – the purchase (or sale) of two puts and a call on a stock that have the same exercise price and expiration date.
    e. Straps – the purchase (or sale) of a put and two calls on a stock that have the same exercise price and expiration date.
    f. Spread – a combination of two or more call (or puts) on the same stock that have differing prices or times to expiration. There are many variations of spreads and the options can be either purchased or sold.
    g. Collar – selling an out of the money call and using the proceeds to purchase an out of the money put.

Chapter 21 Answers
Option Valuation

1. When S_T = $65, it would not make sense to exercise the put and P = $0 (the put expires worthless). However, when S_T = $45, the put would be exercised for a profit of $10 (P = $10). Thus the range of P across the two states is $10 – 0 = $10. The hedge ratio is the change in the value of the put divided by the change in value of the stock, or H = $(P_u – P_d)$ / $(uS_0 – dS_0)$ = ($0 – $10) / ($65 – $45) = –0.50.

2. a. If the stock's price is $70 in one year the call will be exercised and its value will be $70 – 60 = $10. If the stock price is $30 in one year the call will expire worthless. The value trees are shown below.

| Stock's Value | Call Option's Value |

b. The hedge ratio equals the spread in the option values divided by the spread in the stock values.

$$H = \frac{C_u - C_d}{u\,S_0 - d\,S_0} = \frac{10 - 0}{70 - 30} = 0.25$$

c. You would purchase 0.25 shares of stock and write (sell) one call option.
d. The value of your portfolio will be $7.50 in either case.

Stock Value	$70 × 0.25 = $17.50	$30 × 0.25 = $7.50
Obligation from Call written	–$10.00	$0.00
Net Payoff	$7.50	$7.50

e. The present value is $7.50/1.09 = $6.88.
f. The value of the portfolio must equal the present value of its net payoff. The portfolio consists of 0.25 shares of stock held long and one call option written. Its value equals $0.25S_0 – C_0$ = 0.25($50) – C_0 = $6.88, so C_0 = $5.62.

3. Based on your answer to problem 2, the call option is overpriced, so you should sell it and buy the stock. You can sell four call options (1/.25) and receive 4 × $6.20 = $24,80. You can borrow the price of the stock minus the proceeds of the calls' sale = $50 – 24.80 = $25.20, and buy one share of stock for $50. Your net cash outflow is zero ($24.80 + 25.20 - 50).

In one year, if the stock's price is $30 the call options will expire worthless and you will have no obligation. The stock will be worth $30 and you will need to repay $25.20 × 1.09 = $27.47. Your net cash flow will be $2.53 ($30 – 27.47).

If the stock's price is $70 in one year, the call options you sold will be exercised and you will lose $70 – 60 = $10 per option, for a total loss of $40. Your stock will be worth $70 and you will repay your loan with an outflow of $27.47. Your net cash flow will be $2.53 ($70 – 40 – 27.47).

This represents an arbitrage opportunity because you will have earned a profit of $2.53 with no risk and a zero initial outlay. This opportunity should not exist if the markets are in equilibrium.

		Cash Flow in One Year	
	Initial Cash Flow	S = $30	S = $70
Sell 4 options	$24.80	$0.00	–$40.00
Buy 1 share	–$50.00	$30.00	$70.00
Borrow $25.20 @ 9%	$25.20	–$27.47	–$27.47
Total CF	$0.00	$2.53	$2.53

4. In the Black-Scholes option pricing model,
   a. The risk-free interest rate is assumed to be constant over the life of the option.
   b. Stock price volatility is assumed to be constant over the life of the option.
   c. No assumption is necessary about the expected rate of return on the stock – it is implicitly included in the formula through the stock price.
   d. The dividend yield is constant and continuous over the life of the option.
   e. The stock's price is continuous, with no sudden jumps in value.

5. The Black-Scholes Option Pricing Model states that the value of a call option can be calculated as:

$$C0 = S0\ N(d1) - x\ e\text{-}rT\ N(d2)$$
$$d1 = [(\ln S0 / X) + (r + \sigma2 / 2)(T)] / (\sigma \sqrt{T})$$
$$d2 = d1 - \sigma \sqrt{T}$$

$N(d_1)$ and $N(d_2)$ are found in table 21.2 in the text from the computed values of d_1 and d_2, or by using the NORMSDIST Excel function.

Therefore, start by computing d1 and d2. d1 = {[ln (70/75) + (.06 + .45²/2) 1} / .45(1) = {−.06899 + .16125} / .45 = .2050.
d2 =.2050 − .45(1) = −.2450

Therefore, N(d1) and N(d2) (using Excel) are 0.5812 and 0.4032, respectively.

The value of the call is C = ($70)(0.5812) − ($75)(e-0.06(1))(0.4032) = $40.68 − 28.48 = $12.20.

6. The intrinsic value of the in-the-money call is the strike price minus the market price or $52 − 44 = $8.

7. The time value is the premium minus the intrinsic value or $10 − 8 = $2.

8. The elasticity of an option is the percentage change in option price per percentage change in stock price. Remember that the delta (hedge ratio) is the change in option price for a $1 change in stock price. Therefore, the percent change in option price is (.5)($1)/$10.00 = 5.0%. The percentage change in stock price is $1/$52.00 = 1.923%. The elasticity would be (5%/1.923%) = 2.60.

9. Put-call parity says that $P = C + Xe^{-rT} − S_0$. Therefore, rearranging and inserting known values gives: $P = \$10 + 44/e^{-(.06)(.5)} − 52 = \$10 + (44/1.0305) − 52 = \$0.70$.

10. The hedge ratio, delta, indicates that the option's value will change by $0.60 for every $1 change in the stock price. For a $1 change, Portfolio A will have a change of $200 on the 200 shares of stock and $0.6(100) = $60 on the call options. So Portfolio A will have a total change of $260.
Portfolio B will have a change of $250 on the 250 shares of stock for every $1 change in the stock's price.
Therefore, Portfolio A has a higher dollar exposure change.

11. If stock price declined by $1, the value of the stock would decline by $500 and the value of the calls would decrease by [$1(300)(0.6)] = $180, for a total loss of $680.

12. The call hedge ratio = $N(d_1)$ and the put hedge ratio = $N(d_1) − 1$. Therefore, the put hedge ratio is 0.7 − 1.0 = −0.3.

13. The elasticity of an option is the percentage change in option price per percentage change in stock price. Remember that the delta (hedge ratio) is the change in option price for a $1 change in stock price. Therefore, the percentage change in option price is $((.4)(\$1)) / \$4.00 = -10\%$. The percentage change in the stock price is $(\$1) / \$39.00 = 2.5641\%$. The elasticity of the put option is $(-10\% / 2.5641\%) = -3.90$.

14. Most of the factors in the Black-Scholes model are easily observable, except for the standard deviation of the stock's returns. This must be estimated from historical data or from scenario analysis or from the prices of other options. The difference between the values is most likely to be due to different estimates of the standard deviation. For example, if different time periods were used different standard deviations would result.

15. Dynamic, or delta, hedging is the constant updating of the hedge ratio, which results in portfolio adjustments to adjust hedge positions. As the hedge ratio changes, portfolio insurers will buy or sell stock index futures to protect their portfolios from large losses in value. When the market falls, traders might sell a large volume of futures contracts, which can exacerbate the decline. This makes the market more volatile than it would have been without the adjustments in the portfolios. There is evidence that market volatility has increased due to delta hedging.

16. Define the following terms:
    a. gamma – the sensitivity of the delta to the stock price.
    b. delta neutral – when the portfolio has no tendency to change in value as the stock prices of the underlying stocks change.
    c. volatility risk – the risk incurred from unpredictable changes in volatility.
    d. implied volatility – the volatility level from the stock that the option price implies. Computed by solving the Black-Scholes option-pricing model for implied standard deviation.
    e. delta or hedge ratio – the change in the price of an option for a $1 increase in stock price.

17. The longer the time to expiration, the higher the premium. This occurs because the probability that an option can be exercised profitably increases (more time for the stock price to change). The greater the volatility of the underlying stock, the greater the option premium. This is because the higher volatility increases the probability of the option becoming more valuable (e. g., move from an out of the money to an in the money option, or become more in the money). For call options, the lower the exercise price, the more valuable the option, because the option owner can buy the stock at a lower price. For a put option, the lower the exercise price, the less valuable the option. This is because the owner of the option may be required to sell the stock at a lower than market price.

Chapter 22 Answers
Futures Markets

1. The definitions are:
    a. futures price – the amount the buyer of the futures contract agrees to pay to purchase the underlying asset at the maturity date. The seller of the contract agrees to deliver the underlying asset for this price.
    b. settlement price – a representative value of the contract during its last few minutes of trading during the day.
    c. spot price – the current price of the underlying asset in the today's (spot) market.
    d. reversing trade – the trade that will cause the net position in a futures contract to be zero. For someone who currently holds a long position (bought a futures contract), the reversing trade would consist of the sale of an identical contract. For someone who currently holds a short position, the reversing trade would consist of the purchase of an identical contract.
    e. marking to market – the practice of recalculating the value of the contract each day based on current market prices.
    f. basis – the difference between the futures price and the spot price.

2. The clearinghouse puts itself between the buyer and the seller of a futures contract, eliminating the need for individuals to interact and guaranteeing that the contract will be fulfilled. When an individual takes a long position in a futures contract, the clearinghouse is the seller, and when an individual takes a short position the clearinghouse is the buyer. The clearinghouse has the obligation to sell the underlying asset to the holder of the long position and to buy the underlying asset from the holder of the short position.

    If the holder of the long position fails to buy or the holder of the short position fails to deliver, it is the clearinghouse that bears the loss. To minimize the chances of this happening, the clearinghouse marks all accounts to market on a daily basis. If the holder of a long position wants to eliminate the obligation to buy the asset, he can sell an identical futures contract and the clearinghouse will net his position to zero. Similarly, the holder of a short position who wants to eliminate the obligation to deliver the asset can buy an identical futures contract.

3. Based on the information:
    a. The contract is traded on the New York Board of Trade (NYBOT).
    b. The current total value of a position in the contract based on the settle price equals 174.00 cents/lb.(or $1.74/lb.) times 15,000 pounds = $26,100.
    c. Today's settle price is 0.95 higher than the previous day's settle price, so the previous day's settle price was 174.00 – 0.95 = 173.05 cents/lb. (or $1.7305/lb.).

d. The maximum price that was paid for the contract during its lifetime was 176.95 cents/lb. times 15,000 pounds = $26.542.50.

e. There are 8,946 November orange juice contracts outstanding (the open interest).

f. If you take a short position in the contract you will be responsible for delivering 15,000 pounds of the specified type and quality of orange juice on the third Friday of November unless you offset your position through the purchase of an identical contract before that date. At the time of delivery you would receive the $26,100.

4. The profit for a long position in the futures contract equals the spot price at maturity minus the purchase price (650.00) times the units (100 troy oz.) Since you bought the contract you will have to buy the gold for $650 per oz, or a total of $65,000. You can then sell the gold in the spot market at the prevailing price.

The graph shows that the long futures position will lead to a profit when the spot price at expiration is above the purchase price and a loss when the spot price at expiration is below the purchase price.

Spot Price at Maturity	550.00	600.00	650.00	700.00	750.00
Profit to Long Position	-$10,000	-$5,000	$0	$5,000	$10,000

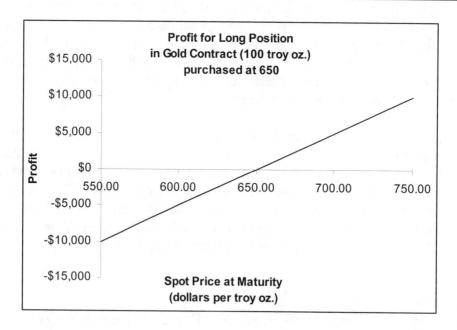

5. Each T-bond contract calls for delivery of $100,000 par value bonds. Since the price is quoted as a percent of par and expressed in 32^{nds} the beginning value is 97.25% of $100,000, or $97,250. The ending value is $98,250. The profit for the long position would be $98,250.00 – $97,250.00 = $1,000.

6. The profit on bonds would be $96,000 – $94,187.50 = $1,812.50. The profit on futures would be $96,468.75 – $96,687.50 = –$218.75. The net profit would be $1,812.50 – $218.75 = $1593.75.

7. You are obligated to buy the silver for $3.15 per oz and can sell it in the market for $3.05 per oz. The profit is the difference between the selling and buying prices times the number of units, or ($3.05 – $3.15)(5,000) = –$500

8. You are obligated to sell the silver for $3.15 per oz and can buy it in the market for $3.05 per oz. The profit is the difference between the selling and buying prices times the number of units, or ($3.15 – $3.05)(5,000) = $500.

9. The gain is the difference between the selling and buying prices times $250 per point, or (1018 – 990)($250) = (28)($250) = $7,000.

10. The value of the futures contract should be the value of the stock index divided by (1 + r_f) minus the dividend, or F = 1200*(1.04) – 45 = 1,203.

11. The total value of the futures contract is the price times the number of units. The listed settle price is 204 cents per bushel, or $2.04 per bushel. So the contract's value is ($2.04)(5,000) = $10,200.

12. The initial margin deposit is the margin percentage times the value of the contract, or (0.10) ($10,200) = $1,020.

13. The answers are shown below. The profit per bushel equals the change in the futures price divided by 100, since the prices are stated in cents. The total value of the contract equals (futures price divided by 100) times 5,000, since the contract size is 5,000 bushels. The mark-to-market settlement equals the change in the value of the contract since you hold the long position.

Day	Futures Price	Profit/Loss per bu.	Total Value of Contract	Mark-to-Market Settlement
0	204.0	n.a.	$10,200	n.a.
1	204.6	$0.006	$10,230	$30
2	206.0	$0.014	$10,300	$70
3	203.9	-$0.021	$10,195	–$105

14. The contract is marked to market daily and profits or losses are posted in the account. The marking-to-market process protects the clearinghouse because the margin percentage is calculated daily and if it falls below the maintenance margin a margin call will be issued. If the investor doesn't meet the call, the clearinghouse can close out enough of the trader's position to restore the margin.

15. You will need to sell 5 futures contracts, each with a face value of $100,000, to hedge the $500,000 of T-notes that you hold.
    The value of the T-notes in 6 months will equal the price (stated as a percentage of par) times the face value of the notes. For example, if the price of the T-notes equals 94 in 6 months, they will be worth 94 percent times $500,000 = $470,000. Since you are selling the futures contracts at 104, you can sell the holder $100,000 of T-notes in 6 months for 104% × $100,000 = $104,000 per contract, for a total of $520,000. The profit on the futures contract will equal $104,000 minus the value of the T-notes at the end of 6 months. So if T-notes are selling at 94 in 6 months, the profit from futures position will be $104,000 – 94,000 = $10,000 per contract, for a total of $50,000.

    Continuing the calculations for an ending value of 94, the total value of what you hold at the end of 6 months will be $470,000 + 50,000 = $520,000.
    The other calculations are done in a similar way. The results are summarized in the table below. Note that the hedge is effective because the total value of the T-notes held and the profit from the short futures position equals $520,000 regardless of the price of the T-notes in six months.

	T-Note Price in 6 months		
	94	104	114
Value of T-note Holdings	$470,000	$520,000	$570,000
Profits or Losses from Futures	$50,000	$0	–$50,000
Total Value	$520,000	$520,000	$520,000

16. A trader that takes a long position is committing to purchase the commodity at the maturity date. A trader that takes a short position is committing to sell the commodity at the maturity date.

17. The convergence property states that the spot price and futures price must be equal (converge) at maturity. This is necessarily true or arbitrage would occur. Contango, normal backwardation, and the expectation hypothesis refer to the relationship between the futures price and the expected value of the spot price at maturity. The expectation hypothesis states that the current futures price is the expected future spot price. Thus, the expected profit to this position is zero. Normal backwardation assumes that most commodities traders are natural hedgers who desire to shed risk. To induce speculators to bear the risk, the futures price must be below the expected future spot price. Thus, if expectations were correct, the speculator would earn a profit $[E(P_T - F_0)]$. Because futures are a zero sum game, the speculators profit equals the hedger's loss. The hedger is willing to incur the loss to shed risk. This is similar to purchasing insurance. Contango is the opposite of normal backwardation and posits that the natural hedgers are the purchasers (rather then sellers) of the commodity. Thus, hedgers would pay a premium to shed risk and the futures price will be above the expected future spot price.

Chapter 23 Answers
Futures, Swaps, and Risk Management

1. Your profit is the selling price minus the buying price times $250 or (–$950 + $922) (250) = –$7,000.

2. Your profit is the selling price minus the buying price times $250 times the number of contracts or ($925 – $884) (250) (4) = $41,000.

3. The new exchange rate should be the current rate times [(1 + home interest rate) / (1 + foreign interest rate)]^T, where T is the number of years.

$$F_0 = E_0 \left(\frac{1 + r_{US}}{1 + r_{SING}} \right)^T = \$0.633 \left(\frac{1.04}{1.08} \right)^{0.25} = \$0.6271 \text{ US per \$1 Singapore}$$

4. The new exchange rate should be the current rate times (1 + home interest rate) divided by (1 + foreign interest rate) or (1.04 / 1.03) ($0.52 /A$) = $0.5250 /A$.

5. The futures contract offers a bargain compared to what it should be, so buy it. To do this, borrow Australian Dollars in Australia, convert them to dollars, lend the proceeds in the United States and enter a long futures position to purchase Australian Dollars in one year at today's futures price. Because of the mispricing, you can earn a riskless profit. The cash flows are shown below.
   For purposes of illustration, start with US$1,000,000. Since the spot exchange rate is 0.52 $US/$AUS, the reciprocal, 1/0.52, can be used to find $AUS/$US. So US$1,000,000 is equivalent to AUS$1,923,076.92.
   a. Borrow AUS$1,923,076.92.
   b. Convert to (US$1,923,076.92)(0.52) = $1,000,000.
   c. Invest in the US for one year and plan to receive (US$1,000,000)(1.04) = $1,040,000 at the end of the year.
   d. Buy futures on Australian Dollars for 0.50. For the sake of illustration, disregard contract size for a moment and assume that we can convert all of our U. S. dollars at the futures price.
   e. Take the proceeds from the US$ investment and convert to AUS$: (US$1,040,000)/(0.50) = AUS$2,080,000.
   f. Pay off the Australian loan: (AUS$1,923,076.92)(1.03) = AUS$1,980,769.23.
   g. Keep your profit of AUS$2,080,000 – AUS$1,980,769.23 = AUS$99,230.77.

6. Borrow US dollars in the United States, convert them to Australian Dollars, lend the proceeds in Australia and enter a futures position to sell Australian Dollars in one year at the current futures price. As an illustration, assume that you start by borrowing either US$1,000,000. The cash flows are shown below.
   a. Borrow US$1,000,000.
   b. Convert to (AUS$$1,000,000)/(0.52) = AUS$1,923,076.92.
   c. Invest in Australia for 1 year and plan to receive (AUS$1,923,076.92)(1.03) = AUS$1,980,769.23 at the end of the year.
   d. Sell futures on Australian Dollars for 0.60. For the sake of illustration, disregard contract size for a moment and assume that we can convert all of our Australian dollars at the futures price.
   e. Take the proceeds from the AUS$ investment and convert to US$: (AUS$1,980,769.23)(0.60) = US$1,188,461.54.
   f. Pay of the US loan: (US$1,000,000)(1.04) = US$1,040,000.
   g. Keep your profit of US$1,188,461.54 – US$1,040,000 = US$148,461.54.

7. The change would represent a drop of (960 – 1025) / 1025 = 6.34% in the index. Given the portfolio's beta, your portfolio would be expected to lose (1.22) (6.34%) = 7.74%. [Note: these answers are shown rounded to two decimal places but should not be rounded in actual calculations.]

8. The dollar value equals the loss of 7.74% times the $1 million portfolio value = $77,365.85. [If your answer is slightly different it may be due to rounding error.]

9. If the S&P 500 drops by 65 points, the buyer of a futures contract would lose (65) ($250) = $16,250 while the seller of the futures would gain (65) ($250) = $16,250.

10. The number of contracts equals the hedge ratio = change in unprotected portfolio value / profit on one futures contract = $77,300/$16,250 = 4.76. You should sell the contract because as the market falls the value of the futures contract will rise and will offset the decline in the portfolio's value.

11. A trader can create a synthetic stock position by buying or selling stock index futures rather than buying or selling all of the individual stocks in the index. This strategy is easy to implement and has much lower transactions costs than the actual purchase of stocks would require. Traders who want to shift in and out of the market as they believe conditions warrant can purchase stock index futures when they are bullish and sell them when they are bearish.

One problem with buying or selling the actual stocks is that it is difficult to execute all transactions simultaneously. Timing problems can lead to ineffective results. The use of stock index futures allows traders to participate in the equities' performance without the actual purchase of equities.

12. a. The current value of your bond portfolio is $1 million since the market rate equals the coupon rate:
N = 20, I/Y = 94.5, PMT = .09 × 1,000,000 = 90,000, FV = 1,000,000
CPT PV ⇒ 1,000,000.

b. The current value of the $1 million face value, 8% delivery bond is $908,714.54:
N = 20, I/Y = 9, PMT = .08 × 1,000,000 = 80,000, FV = 1,000,000
CPT PV ⇒ 908,714.54.

c. If the market rate changes to 10.5% the value of your bond portfolio will be $876,536.37:
N = 20, I/Y = 10.5, PMT = .09 × 1,000,000 = 90,000, FV = 1,000,000
CPT PV ⇒ 876,536.37.
The amount of change is $876,536.37 − 1,000,000 = −$123,463.63.

d. The value of the 8% delivery bond at a market rate of 10.5% is $794,227.28:
N = 20, I/Y = 10.5, PMT = .08 × 1,000,000 = 80,000, FV = 1,000,000
CPT PV ⇒ 794,227.28.
The amount of the change in value on this bond is $794,227.28 − 908,714.54 = −$114,487.27.

e. You would need to short approximately 123,463.63/114,487.27 = 1.08 futures contracts to enact the hedge, since the fall in the price of the 8% bond would approximately equal the profit on the short futures position.

13. Index arbitrage provides a way to exploit mispricing when an actual index futures price is different from its parity value. Parity means that the futures contract price properly reflects the value of the stocks in the index.

If parity is violated, the trader will sell what's overpriced and buy what's underpriced. For example, if the index futures price is too high, the trader will take a short position in the futures contract and buy the stocks in the index. The arbitrage profits will equal the amount by which the futures contract is mispriced. One problem with executing this strategy is that the transactions costs for buying or selling the stocks in the index will diminish, and perhaps completely eliminate the profit.

Program trading is useful because the strategy depends heavily on the ability to conduct all of the stock transactions simultaneously. Without this feature the temporary mispricings could vanish and the opportunity for arbitrage would disappear. With program trading, the traders can send the entire order through the NYSE SuperDot system via computer to increase the odds of all of the orders being executed at the same time.

14. If interest rates rise the value of the portfolio will fall because bond prices move inversely with interest rates. However, it would be very expensive to sell the bonds. You can hold the bonds and use an interest rate swap to exchange the cash flows associated with the fixed-rate bonds for cash flows based on a floating rate. If you are correct, and interest rates rise, the cash flows from the floating rate will offset the decline in the bond portfolio's value. If you are incorrect, and interest rates fall, you will lose money due to lower cash flows from the floating rate, but this will be offset by an increase in the value of the bond portfolio.

The calculations are shown in the table below, which assumes a starting LIBOR rate equal to the coupon rate of the bonds. The table entries show what will happen if the LIBOR rate rises or falls by 0.5%.

	LIBOR Rate		
	5.90%	6.40%	6.90%
Interest Income on Portfolio	$3,200,000	$3,200,000	$3,200,000
Cash Flow from Swap	- 250,000	0	250,000
Total Cash Flow	$2,950,000	$3,200,000	$3,450,000

Interest income on the portfolio = .064 x $50,000,000 = $3,200,000
Cash flow from swap = (Ending LIBOR − .064) * $50,000,000
Total cash flow = interest income on the portfolio + cash flow from swap

15. Explain the relationship between covered interest arbitrage and interest rate parity. How do these relate to foreign exchange rates?

16. Foreign currencies are quoted as either direct or indirect quotes. Explain what each quote means and explain the relationship between the two quotes.

Chapter 24 Answers
Portfolio Performance Evaluation

1. First, calculate the return for each year as the change in price divided by the beginning price. The calculations for the returns are shown below.
   year 1:(46 – 42) / 42 = 9.52%, year 2:(54 – 46) / 46 =17.39%, year 3:(62–54) / 54 = 14.81%, year 4: = (59-62) / 62 = –4.84%.
   To compute the geometric average return for the period, add one to each period's return, which gives the return relative. Then find the product of these. Raise the product to the power 1 / n and subtract 1. The geometric return equals [(1.0952)(1.1739)(1.1481)(0.9516)]1 / 4 – 1.0 = 8.87%.

Time	Price	Return	Return Relative
0	$42.00		
1	$46.00	9.52%	1.0952
2	$54.00	17.39%	1.1739
3	$62.00	14.81%	1.1481
4	$59.00	–4.84%	0.9516
	Geometric Return =		**8.87%**

2. The time-weighted return is the geometric average of the annual returns. The return for year 1 is ($46 + $2 – $42) / $42 = 14.29%. The return for year 2 is ($54.00 + $2 – $46) / $46 = 21.74%. The geometric average is $[(1.1429)(1.2174)]^{0.5} - 1 = 17.95\%$.

3. The dollar-weighted return is the internal rate of return (IRR) of the investment. The initial outflow is (–$42). Cash flow 1 is –$44 (the $46 stock price minus the $2 dividend), and cash flow 2 is $112 (two times the stock price plus two times the dividend). Therefore, $-\$42 = -\$44 / (1 + r) + \$112 / (1 + r)^2$ and r = 19.11%.

4. For the recent one-year period, the return on the 5th percentile portfolio (the solid bottom line) was about 2%. The 25th percentile portfolio (the lowest of the dashed lines) returned about 2.75%, the 50th percentile portfolio (the middle dashed line) returned about 4.3%, the 75th percentile portfolio (the highest dashed line) returned approximately 6%, and the 95th percentile portfolio (the solid upper line) returned about 7%. Your portfolio earned a return of about 5.2%, which placed you in approximately the 62nd percentile.

   Over the past five years, the municipal funds' return percentiles were 3% (5th percentile), 3.8% (25th percentile), 5.2% (50th percentile), 7% (75th percentile), and 8% (95th percentile). During the five-year period, you fared worse. Your funds averaged a 4.2% return, which placed you in about the 36th percentile of municipal bond funds.

5. The Sharpe measure is the return on the portfolio minus the risk-free rate divided by the standard deviation of the portfolio's returns. Therefore, $(.14 - .05) / .26 = .3462$

6. The Treynor measure is the return on the portfolio minus the risk-free rate divided by the beta of the portfolio's returns. Therefore, the Treynor measure is $(.14 - .05) / 1.2 = .075$.

7. The Jensen measure is the alpha from the CAPM equation $\alpha_{GSF} = [R_{GSF} - (R_f + \beta_{GSF}(R_M - R_f)]$. Therefore, Guardian's alpha equals $.14 - [.05 + 1.2 (.10 - .05)] = .0300 = 3.00\%$.

8. The information ratio is the alpha divided by the residual standard deviation. We can use the alpha that we computed for Jensen's measure, so $\alpha_{GSF} / \sigma(e_{GSF}) = 3\% / 4\% = 0.75$, or 75.00%

9. To compute the M^2 measure, you must find the proportion of funds allocated to the risky and risk-free asset that will cause the risks (standard deviations) of the market and the hypothetical portfolio (P*) to be equal. The proportion of P in P* should be $\sigma_M / \sigma_P = 0.21 / 0.26 = .8077$ and the proportion of the risk-free asset in P* should be $(1 - .8077) = .1923$

    Next, we need to calculate the expected return of hypothetical portfolio P* given the returns of the assets and the weights calculated above. In this case, $(.8077)(14\%) + (.1923)(5\%) = 12.27\%$.

    Finally, the M2 measure is the return of P* minus the return on the market $(12.27\% - 10\%) = 2.27\%$.

10. The graph is shown below. It is clear that portfolios P and P* are on a CAL that has a higher reward-to-volatility ratio than the market portfolio. The client would be better off holding one of these rather than a market index fund.

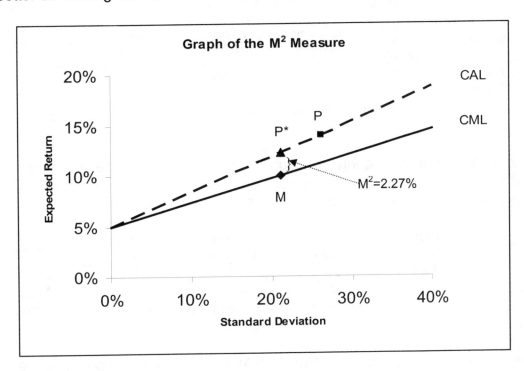

11. The Sharpe measure or the M^2 measure should be used when total risk is relevant. If all of an investor's assets are handled by one manager, then both systematic risk and unique risk are important. The manager should try to diversify effectively within the portfolio and her performance should be judged based on excess return relative to total volatility.

The Treynor measure or the Jensen measure is appropriate when there is diversification of assets among many managers. Individual managers do not need to focus on diversification within the portfolio they manage because it is a small component of an overall portfolio. In this case, systematic risk is relevant and excess returns relative to beta may be used to gauge performance.

12. The total excess return is the return on the portfolio minus the return of the bogey, or 9% − 6.5% = 2.5%.

13. The excess return due to asset allocation can be expressed as the sum, over all asset classes, of the weight in the portfolio minus the weight in the index times the return on the index. The table below shows the results of the calculations.

Market	Growth Fund Weight	Benchmark Weight	Excess Weight	Market Return	Contribution
Bonds	20%	50%	–30%	5%	–1.50%
Stocks	80%	50%	30%	10%	3.00%
		contribution of asset allocation across markets			1.50%

14. The excess return to security selection can be expressed as the sum, over all asset classes, of the return on the portfolio minus return on the index times the weight in the portfolio. The table below shows the results of the calculations.

Market	Portfolio Performance	Index Performance	Excess Performance	Portfolio Weight	Contribution
Bonds	4%	5%	–1%	20%	–0.20%
Stocks	9%	10%	–1%	80%	–0.80%
		contribution of selection within markets			–1.00%

15. The Morningstar Risk-Adjusted Rating (RAR) system provides performance measures that are similar to the mean-variance measures. The well-known star measure ranks mutual funds into one of five categories. The funds with the best RARs earn five stars; the funds with the worst RARs earn one star.

To determine how many stars a fund should earn Morningstar adjusts the returns for load fees, then calculates the fund's returns and a risk measure based on the fund's performance during its worst years. The funds are segregated into style groups based on fund objectives and portfolio characteristics like market capitalization and financial ratios.

Next the funds are ranked according to their RARs. Stars are awarded according to the funds' percentile rankings. Funds in the 0-10th percentiles get 1 star. Funds in the 10th through 32.5th percentiles get 2 stars, etc., up to 5 stars for funds in the 90-100th percentiles.

The Morningstar measure is very well known and respected among both professional and small investors.

16. Evaluating the performance of hedge funds presents several practical challenges. First, the risk profile (total volatility and exposure to relevant systematic factors) changes rapidly. Secondly, large investments in illiquid assets pose two problems. Illiquid assets are difficult to accurately price (have stale prices) which complicates calculating a rate or return. Additionally, it is difficult to disentangle the liquidity premium from true alpha. Third, survivorship bias can be severe because hedge finds disappear at a much greater rate than mutual funds. Finally, hedge funds pursue strategies that provide expected profits over a long period of time but expose the fund to infrequent but severe losses.

17. The Jensen measure (alpha) is computed in practice by running the following ordinary least squares regression (OLS)
$$R_p - R_f = \alpha + \beta (R_m - R_f).$$
This equation can be thought of as equivalent to the equation for a straight line. A distinct advantage of using OLS regression techniques to compute alpha is that the estimated alpha can be subjected to the hypothesis test that it equals zero. Thus, we could tell is a positive (negative) alpha was good (bad) in a statistical sense. Unfortunately, active management such as market timing clouds the issue because the OLS technique assumes beta is constant (stable). When portfolio managers time the market (correctly or incorrectly), the portfolio beta changes. This change in beta causes the characteristic line to be curvilinear rather than linear. Thus, the Jensen measure fails to fully evaluate performance. Two techniques that have been widely accepted to deal with the evaluation of market timing are the Treynor-Mazuy (1966) and the Henriksson-Merton (1981) methods. Each starts with the basic Jensen model but each adds an additional term to capture the timing element. The equations and extended discussion of these models is provided in section 24.4 of the textbook.

Chapter 25 Answers
International Diversification

1. According to the World Bank, an emerging market is one with per capita income of less than $10,000 (as of 2005). A developed market is one with per capita income of more than $10,000.

   The top six developed countries made up 78.5% of world capitalization in 2000, but only 71.6% in 2005. A passive portfolio management strategy with allocations to the equities of these six countries might be sufficiently diversified for a passive investor.

   An active strategy, however, would require more analysis so that securities could be chosen carefully. Securities or indexes with prospects for better performance would be favored, and it is likely that emerging countries would be well represented in the actively managed portfolio.

2. The major requirement is a developed code of business laws, institutions, and regulation that allows citizens to legally own, capitalize, and trade capital assets. Countries whose capital markets are well developed have higher levels of economic well-being. In one analysis the relationship between per capita GDP and market capitalization as a percentage of GDP had a regression coefficient of .91. Each increase of 1% in the ratio of market capitalization to GDP brings about an average increase of .91% in per capita GDP. Almost all developed countries and a few emerging markets fell above the regression line relating these two factors. Emerging countries that fell below the regression line tended to have problems such as unstable political environments and/or government policies that constrained private sector activities.

3. The return to a US investor can be expressed as $r(US) = [1 + r_f(UK)] (E_1 / E_0) - 1$. Inserting known values and solving gives: $(1.06) (1.62 / 1.66) - 1 = 3.45\%$.

4. The return to a U. S. investor can be expressed as $1 + r_f(US) = [1 + r_f(UK)] (F_0 / E_0)$ so this problem can be expressed as $1.04 = (1 + r_f(UK)(1.57/1.66) - 1$. Inserting known values and solving gives: $r_f(UK) = 9.96\%$.

5. The return to a U. S. investor consists of the Canadian interest rate plus the gain or loss of foreign exchange. This can be expressed as $1.05(0.79 / 0.75) - 1 = r(US)$. Therefore, $r(US) = 10.6\%$.

6. Again, it is appropriate to start with the basic equation where the return to a U. S. investor can be expressed as $r(US) = [1 + r(UK)](F_0/E_0) - 1$. Inserting known values gives: $1.04/1.06 = x/1.62$ and solving gives $x = 1.5894$.

7. It is appropriate to start with the basic equation where the return to a U. S. investor can be expressed as $r(US) = [1 + r(Can)](F_0/E_0) - 1$. Inserting known values gives: $1.035 = [(\$0.76/\$0.75)(1 + r)] - 1$. Therefore, $r = 2.14\%$.

8. The return on the portfolio would be the weighted average of the returns of the two countries or $12\%(0.5) + 14\%(0.5) = 13\%$.

9. The standard deviation of a portfolio is the square root of its variance and can be expressed as $\sigma_P = [(0.5)^2(19)^2 + (0.5)^2(22)^2 + 2(0.5)(0.5)(1.7)]^{1/2} = 14.56\%$.

10. Your initial investment in US dollars was the number of pounds invested times the cost of pounds or $(12,000)(\$1.60) = \$19,200$. Your gain is the change in the dollar value of the investment, which is number of pounds the securities as now worth times the current value of pounds or $(14,625)(1.63) = \$23,838.75$. The return is the change in the value of the securities (in dollar terms) divided by the initial investment or $(\$23,838.75 - \$19,200)/\$19,200 = 0.2416 = 24.16\%$.

11. The factors considered fall into three categories: political risk variables, financial risk variables, and economic risk variables.

    Political risk variables include government stability, socioeconomic conditions, investment profile, internal conflicts, external conflicts, level of corruption, the role of the military in politics, religious tensions, law and order, ethnic tensions, democratic accountability, and bureaucracy quality.

    Financial risk variables include foreign debt as a percent of Gross Domestic Product (GDP), foreign debt service as a percent of GDP, the current account as a percentage of exports, net liquidity in months of imports, and exchange rate stability.

    Economic risk variables include GDP per capita, real annual GDP growth, the country's annual inflation rate, budget balance as a percent of GDP, and the current account balance as a percent of GDP.

12. The following factors may be measured to determine the performance of an international portfolio manager.
    (A) Currency selection: a benchmark might be the weighted average of the currency appreciation of the currencies represented in the EAFE portfolio.
    (B) Country selection measures the contribution to performance attributable to investing in the better-performing stock markets of the world. Country selection can be measured as the weighted average of the equity index returns of each country using as weights the share of the manager's portfolio in each country.
    (C) Stock selection ability may be measured as the weighted average of equity returns in excess of the equity index in each country.

13. To calculate overall performance, you need to calculate the total return for both the EAFE and Exotic. The overall return is the sum of the returns from each of the markets. The return on equity in each market equals the weight in each market times the total return in that market. The total return in each market is the return on the equity plus the foreign exchange gain. The calculations are shown below.

    EAFE: $(.35)(13\% + 4\%) + (.15)(22\% - 6\%) + (.50)(16\% + 8\%) = 20.35\%$ and
    Exotic: $(.40)(19\% + 4\%) + (.10)(18\% - 6\%) + (.50)(32\% + 8\%) = 30.40\%$.
    Exotic outperformed the EAFE by $(30.4\% - 20.35\%) = 10.05\%$.

14. The currency selection contribution can be computed by summing the products of the weight in each market by the currency appreciation in that market, or

    EAFE: $(.35)(4\%) + (.15)(-6\%) + (.50)(8\%) = 4.5\%$ appreciation and
    Exotic: $(.40)(4\%) + (.10)(-6\%) + (.50)(8\%) = 5\%$ appreciation.
    Exotic had a gain of $(5\% - 4.5\%) = 0.5\%$ relative to EAFE.

15. The country selection contribution can be computed by summing the products of the weight in each market by the return in that market or

    EAFE: $(.35)(13\%) + (.15)(22\%) + (.50)(16\%) = 15.85\%$ and
    Exotic: $(.40)(13\%) + (.10)(22\%) + (.50)(16\%) = 15.40\%$.
    Exotic had a gain of $(15.40\% - 15.85\%) = -0.45\%$ relative to EAFE. Since the gain is negative, they lost ground relative to EAFE because of country selection.

16. The stock selection contribution can be computed by summing the products of the Exotic funds weight in each market by the difference in the return of the Exotic fund and the EAFE, or $(19\% - 13\%)(.40) + (18\% - 22\%)(.10) + (32\% - 16\%)(.50) = 10\%$.

17. Several observations can be made from the data. First, both local currency and U.S. dollar returns varied considerably among countries during this period. In addition, the standard deviations of returns (both local currency and U.S. dollar) varied considerably among countries. Finally, both local currency and U.S. dollar correlations are low in many cases. One may conclude from this data that it may be riskier to hold one country's equity that it is to hold a diversified portfolio of equities. Moreover, the return of a well-diversified portfolio may be higher. If you compare these returns for China with the 2007 returns, it will highlight the fact that losers in one period may be winners in the next. Thus, diversification can "smooth" the highs and lows.

Chapter 26 Answers
Hedge Funds

1. The five major categories of differences are transparency, investors, investment strategies, liquidity, and compensation structure. Mutual funds are more highly regulated by the SEC and thus are required to be far more transparent. Hedge funds provide only minimal information about portfolio composition or strategy. Investors in hedge funds differ in that investment minimums were traditionally set at $250,000 to $1,000,000. While newer hedge funds are starting to reduce the minimum investment to $25,000, this minimum is outside the reach of many mutual fund investors. Mutual funds must provide an investment strategy and are restricted in the use of leverage, short selling, and in their use of derivatives. However, hedge funds are less restricted and frequently make large bets that can results in large losses over the short term. Mutual funds are liquid and investors can redeem shares at NAV and have proceeds within seven business days. Conversely, hedge funds often impose lock-up periods as long as several years and require redemption notices of several months even after the lock-up period is over. Thus, hedge funds are less liquid. While mutual funds charge a management fee, hedge funds add an incentive fee as well. This incentive fee is similar to a call option and the portfolio manager receives a "performance" bonus if the portfolio outperforms the chosen benchmark.

2. Directional strategies are bets that one sector will outperform another sector during a given period. Non-directional strategies are designed to exploit temporary misalignments in relative pricing. Non-directional strategies typically involve a long position in one asset and a short position in a related security. An example would be if the yield on mortgage-backed securities were abnormally high compared to Treasury bonds, a hedge fund could short sell the Treasury and buy the mortgage-backed securities. Thus, if relative values returned to normal, the yield on the MBS would decline (and price increase) and the yield on the Treasury would increase (price decrease). Thus, the hedge fund would profit from betting on a decrease in the spread.

3. A market neutral position is one that is designed to exploit relative mispricing within a market, but which is hedged to avoid taking a stance on the direction of the broad market. Relative mispricing can take many forms however; the example used in the chapter of the yield on mortgage-backed securities being abnormally high compared to Treasury bonds is a good one. A hedge fund could short sell the Treasury and buy the mortgage-backed securities. This strategy is market neutral because it is not taking a stand on changes in the level of interest rates in the economy. An increase (or decrease) in the level of interest rates will affect the required yields (and prices) of both securities. Moreover, since the fund has a long and a short position, the gains on one position would offset the losses on the other

position if interest rates changed (*ceteris paribus*). However, these are not risk free strategies simply because market risk has been hedged away. If relative values returned to normal, the yield on the MBS would decline (and price increase) and the yield on the Treasury would increase (price decrease). Thus, the hedge fund would profit from betting on a decrease in the spread. However, if spreads do not return to normal, the fund does not make a large return. Moreover, spreads may widen substantially and remain abnormally wide for an extended period. In addition, if the spread does widen, the fund stands to lose money.

4. The return on the portfolio can be described as:
$$R_{portfolio} = r_f + \beta(r_M - r_f) + e + \alpha$$
Where e is the firm specific risk reflected in the residual.

5. The value of the portfolio if the market rose 5% would be the beginning value of the portfolio multiplied by one plus the return (from question #4 above). The return during the 30 days would be
Return = $0.0025 + 1.12(.05 - 0.0025) + 0 + .02 = 0.0757$ or 7.57%.
Therefore, the value of the portfolio would be
$$1,250,000 (1.0757) = 1,344,625.$$
The dollar gain would be $\$1,344,625 - 1,250,000 = 94,625$

6. If the market fell 10%, The return during the 30 days would be
Return = $0.0025 + 1.12(-.10 - 0.0025) + 0 + .02 = -0.0923$ or -9.23%.
Therefore, the value of the portfolio would be
$$1,250,000 (0.9077) = 1,134,625.$$
The dollar loss would be $\$1,134,625 - 1,250,000 = 115,375$

7. The hedge ratio can be computed as $[\$1,250,000 / (1,400 \times \$250)] \times 1.12 = 4$ contracts. Thus, the portfolio can be hedged by selling 4 futures contacts on the S&P 500.

8. If the market rose 5%, the gain on the futures position would be
(Fo – F1) × \$250 × 4 contracts or
$(1,400 – [1,400 \times 1.05] \times \$250) \times 4$ contracts
$(\$1,400 – \$1,470) \times \$250 \times 4 = -70,000.$

9. If the market fell 10%, the gain on the futures position would be
(Fo – F1) × \$250 × 4 contracts or
$(1,400 – [1,100 \times .9] \times \$250) \times 4$ contracts
$(\$1,400 – \$1,260) \times \$250 \times 4 = 140,000.$

10. Gain on portfolio   94,625
     Loss on futures position   −70,000
     Change in wealth   24,625
     Return = 24,625 / 1,250,000 = 1.97% (roughly the alpha of the portfolio, 2%).

11. Loss on portfolio   −115,375
     Gain on futures position   140,000
     Change in wealth   24,625
     Return = 24,625 / 1,250,000 = 1.97% (roughly the alpha of the portfolio, 2%).

12. By creating a market neutral hedge, the 2% per month alpha has been protected (isolated) from movements in the broad market. This is alpha portability.

13. The portfolio is not riskless! The alpha is not a sure thing and firm specific factors may affect portfolio returns. The portfolio is only protected from market risk.

Chapter 27 Answers
The Theory of Active Portfolio Management

There are no problems for Chapter 27

Chapter 28 Answers
Investment Policy and the Framework of the CFA Institute

1. The four major steps in making an investment decision are specifying objectives, specifying constraints, formulating policy, and monitoring and updating the portfolio as needed.

2. The central focus of portfolio objectives must be on the risk-return trade off. In dealing with the risk-return tradeoff, the risk-tolerance of the investor is crucial. You may want to refer to the discussion on risk aversion and utility in chapter 6 to see why it is important to consider these two factors.

3. Constraints consist of factors relevant to the specific investor, whether the investor is a person or a firm. These constraints consist of factors such as the investor's liquidity needs, investment horizon, legal regulations, tax situation, and unique needs.

4. The steps in determining asset allocation are:
   a. determining the asset classes to be included in the portfolio (such as money market instruments, fixed income securities, stocks, real estate, precious metals, and others)
   b. developing expectations concerning the return and risk characteristics of the various investment options over the investment horizon
   c. deriving the efficient frontier, which shows the maximum possible expected return for each level of risk
   d. finding the optimal asset mix, which involves combining the efficient frontier data with the constraints the investor faces

5. As an individual, the most important factor is the stage in one's life cycle. The stage in the investor's life cycle is important because it is generally associated with important factors such as liquidity needs and investment horizon.

6. Mutual funds have relatively low liquidity needs. The only time liquidity needs would increase for mutual funds is when redemptions increase rapidly. Typically, the funds have new money coming in that can be invested or used to meet redemption needs.

   Pension funds' liquidity needs depend on the age of the work force. If the work force consists of mostly young workers the liquidity needs will be low. If there are mostly older workers who are nearing or in retirement, then liquidity needs will be high since funds will need to be available for payouts.

Endowment funds typically have low liquidity needs since they pay out a relatively small portion of their assets. Endowments usually bring in contributions on a regular basis, increasing the fund's value.

7. The "prudent investor rule" is a standard that provides general guidelines to professionals who manage money on behalf of other people. The managers have a fiduciary responsibility to act in the best interests of the parties whose money they manage. The rule does not specifically list activities that are acceptable or forbidden, but restricts investments to those assets that would be chosen by a prudent investor.

    If the money manager takes excessive risks with the funds he or she may be sued by the parties whose money is being managed. This is true even if the returns were high relative to the market average. Professional money managers need to document and justify their decisions so that they can defend them in a court of law if necessary.

8. a. A whole-life insurance policy has both a benefit which is payable to the beneficiary at the death of the insured and a savings plan. The policyholder can withdraw the cash value of the policy or borrow against it.
    b. Term life insurance consists of only a death benefit. There is no buildup of cash value.
    c. A variable life insurance policy offers a death benefit and a savings component, where the policyholder may choose from among several mutual funds for investment of the cash value. Earnings on the cash value are not taxed until the money is withdrawn.
    d. A universal life policy contains a feature that allows the policyholder to increase or reduce either the insurance premium or the death benefit as the cash value builds. This type of policy has an interest rate that changes as market rates change. Earnings on the cash value are not taxed until the money is withdrawn.

    The portfolio needs of life insurance companies depend on the types of policies they write. If the amount of the death benefit is linked to inflation, then the company will need to be aware of, and compensate for, inflation risk. Actuarial analyses help in determining the likelihood and the timing of payouts of death benefits. The assumptions incorporated into these analyses are important. Factors such as death rates, return on funds invested, and cash value redemptions are key. A sensitivity analysis can be done to get a range of possible outcomes and the impacts of various outcomes on the company's portfolio.

9. The two basic types of pension plans are the defined contribution plan and the defined benefit plan.

   In a defined contribution plan, the employer makes regular payments into the account on behalf of the employee. There is no guarantee of an amount that will be available for the employee at retirement. The employee bears all of the risk regarding the financial outcome of the plan. The employee may choose from among several different investment funds for the assets and the earnings are not taxed until the funds are withdrawn.

   In a defined benefit plan, the risk of the financial outcome lies with the employer, who has an obligation to pay a fixed amount to the employee in retirement. The amount to be paid is determined by a formula with variables such as the employee's salary and years of service. If there is a shortfall, the firm must make up the difference between what is available in the fund and what is needed to make the required payouts.

10. The seven risks that investors face are:
    a. Market risk (or principal risk) – the risk that the market will decline causing you to loose money that you invested. While some investors may not be forced to withdraw money from the market, retirees may be required to realize capital losses.
    b. Purchasing power risk (inflation risk) – the risk that your investment strategy is too conservative and your money will not grow fast enough to keep pace with inflation. You can relate this to material in Chapter 5. Recall that the realized real rate of return can be negative if the inflation rate exceeded the nominal rate of interest during a previous period.
    c. Interest-rate risk – occurs if interest rates decline and you desire to reinvest the money. In addition, investments in variable rate vehicles will produce lower payment streams if interest rates adjust downward.
    d. Timing risk – the chance that an investment will not be doing well at the particular time that you need the money. For example, the S&P 500 index falls 15% and you are completely invested in an S&P 500 index fund. Asset allocation can reduce, but not eliminate, this risk.
    e. Liquidity risk – the risk that an asset cannot be liquidated quickly at a fair price. This is often associated with investments in illiquid (not exchange traded) assets. This may include art, antiques, collectables, etc.
    f. Political risk – the prospect that government decisions will affect the value of your portfolio.
    g. Societal risk (world event risk) – the risk that some world event or act of nature will cause poor investment performance during some period.

    Other potential risks include foreign exchange risk and/or credit risk.

11. To solve this problem, it is easiest to use your financial calculator. Given the data, PV = –650,000, I/Y = 7.5, N = 18, FV = 0, Compute PMT ⇒ 66,968.82. [Remember the interpretation of the positive and negative signs. You are investing the $650,000, so it is treated as an outflow and has a negative sign. The annuity payments will be inflows so the PMT has a positive sign.]

12. A variable annuity guarantees a minimum payment, but you may get higher payments if the annuity earns a return that is higher than expected. We can start by using the hypothetical constant annual benefit payment we found in problem 5, which was $66,968.82. This payment is then adjusted due to the higher realized return. To make the adjustment, multiply the hypothetical constant benefit payment by the ratio [(1 + actual return) / (1 + expected return)]. So the starting payment in this case would be $66,968.82 (1.09 / 1.075) = $67,903.27.

13. The safe account has (.25)($278,000) = $69,500 and the risky account has (.75)($278,000) = $208,500.

14. The safe account gets (.25)($2,500 + 2,500) = $1,250 and the risky account gets (.75)($2,500 + 2,500) = $3,750.

15. Richard has 14 years until he retires. The value in the safe account in 14 years will be the future value of the present amount in the safe account ($69,500) plus the future value of the $1,250 annuity in 14 years. The interest rate for both is the risk-free rate that he is guaranteed (3%). The entries for the financial calculator are: N = 14, I/Y = 3, PV = – 69,500, PMT = –1,250, Compute FV ⇒ $126,482.89.

16. The expected value in the risky account in 14 years will be the future value of the present amount in the risky account ($208,500) plus the future value of the $3,750 annuity in 14 years. The rate of return for both is the expected rate of return (11%). The entries for the financial calculator are: N = 14, I/Y = 11, PV = –208,500, PMT = –3,750, Compute FV ⇒ $1,011,582.89.

17. a. The plan needs to have the present value of the obligation amount: N = 23, I/Y = 9, PMT = 0, FV = 25,000,000, CPT PV ⇒ 3,444,534.64. You would need to have $3,444,534.64 on deposit today to meet the goal.
     b. To answer this question, we need to break the calculation into two parts. The present value of the annuity obligation as of time 6 (one period before it starts) is calculated as
     N = 18, I/Y = 9, PMT = 1,500,000, FV = 0, CPT PV ⇒ 13,133,437.66. The value of this amount today is calculated as
     N = 6, I/Y = 9, PMT = 0, FV = 13,133,437.66, CPT PV ⇒ 7,831,039.77. The account balance should be at least $7,831,039.77 today to meet the goal. Note that in both cases if a return of less than 9% is realized the pension plan will be underfunded.